# Jewish Moroccan Folk Narratives from Israel

# Jewish Folklore and Anthropology Series

*General Editor*
Raphael Patai

*Advisory Editors*

Dan Ben-Amos
University of Pennsylvania

Gedalya Nigal
Bar Ilan University

Jane Gerber
City University of New York

Aliza Shenhar
University of Haifa

Barbara Kirshenblatt-Gimblett
YIVO Institute for Jewish Research

Amnon Shiloah
Hebrew University

*Books in this series*

*The Myth of the Jewish Race,* revised edition, by Raphael Patai and Jennifer Patai, 1989

*The Hebrew Goddess,* third enlarged edition, by Raphael Patai, 1990

*Robert Graves and the Hebrew Myths: A Collaboration,* by Raphael Patai, 1992

*Jewish Musical Traditions,* by Amnon Shiloah, 1992

*The Jews of Kurdistan,* by Erich Brauer, completed and edited by Raphael Patai, 1993

*Jewish Moroccan Folk Narratives from Israel,* by Haya Bar-Itzhak and Aliza Shenhar, 1993

# Jewish
# Moroccan
# Folk
# Narratives
# from Israel

Haya Bar-Itzhak
*and*
Aliza Shenhar

Wayne State University Press    Detroit

### Library of Congress Cataloging-in-Publication Data

Jewish Moroccan folk narratives from Israel/ Haya Bar-Itzhak, Aliza Shenhar :
    translated by Miriam Widmann in collaboration with the authors].
      p.   cm. — (Jewish folklore and anthropology series)
    Includes bibliographical references and index.
    ISBN 0-8143-2442-8 (alk. paper). — ISBN 0-8143-2443-6 (pbk. alk. paper)
    1. Folk literature, Judeo-Arabic—Morocco—Translations into English. 2. Folk
literature, Judeo-Arabic—Morocco—History and criticism. 3. Tales—Morocco.
4. Tales—Israel—Shelomi. 5. Legends, Jewish. 6. Jews,
Moroccan—Israel—Shelomi—Folklore. 7. Shelomi (Israel)—social life and
customs. I. Bar-Itshak, Haya. II. Shenhar-Alroy, Aliza. III. Series.
GR98.J49   1993
398.2'089'9276405694—dc20                                    92-44747

Designer: Mary Krzewinski

Cover art: Mordekhai Malka (front cover). Parokhet, a curtain for the Holy Ark. Y.
Aynhorn collection. Permission of the Israel Museum, Jerusalem (background).

Translated by Miriam Widmann in collaboration with the authors.

THIS BOOK IS
DEDICATED
TO THE
STORY-TELLERS
AND
THEIR FAMILIES

# *Contents*

# CONTENTS

# Contents

# Illustrations:
## Folk Art and Material Culture
## of Moroccan Jews

# ILLUSTRATIONS

# Introduction

In this collection a selection of folk narratives of Moroccan Jews in Israel is presented. The narratives were recorded as part of a research project undertaken in the development town of Shlomi, Israel.[1] An account of the narrator's life and a commentary have been appended to each narrative. The narratives were selected to represent proportionally the number of stories told by each story-teller, to present the different genres of the community, and to represent both female and male story-tellers.

The development town of Shlomi is situated in the west region of the Galilee, not far from the Lebanese border. It is located 12 kilometers from Nahariya and 42 kilometers from Haifa. Shlomi was founded in the 1950s to absorb immigrants arriving during the mass immigration after the establishment of the State of Israel. The settlement is named after Shlomi, father of Ahihud head of the biblical tribe of Asher, in whose territory the town of Shlomi was founded. The first inhabitants of Shlomi were Yemenite and Yugoslavian immigrants who lived in the transit camp constructed in the early 1950s. Conditions in those early years were difficult and the settlers moved on to other settlements. They were replaced by immigrants from North Africa. When we did the field work (1981-1983) most residents, a population of approximately 2,500, were Moroccan Jews, and we recorded the folk narratives from them.

The folk narrative was a feature of Jewish life in Morocco for centuries. Preachers used it when they preached in the synagogue, and narrators used it to teach, educate, and entertain their audi-

---

[1] The narratives are stored in the Israel Folktale Archives (IFA) at the University of Haifa, Israel. IFA was established in the 1950s by Dov Noy. It comprises about 18,000 folk narratives as told by story-tellers from various ethnic groups in Israel.

Shlomi.

ences. The folk narrative had therefore the approval of the bearers of tradition and thousands of listeners for many generations.

As researchers of folklore we tried, by recording the narratives, to make our contribution to the preservation of the heritage of this ethnic group that at the time was changing fast and might in part no longer be available in a few years. But mainly we wanted to test the folk narrative as a dynamic process. On the one hand, these stories were brought to Israel by the narrators from their country of origin. On the other hand, the narratives were narrated by storytellers residing in Shlomi who were constantly in contact with the Israeli culture into which they had been transplanted. What happens to traditional folk literature in this process? What impact does the process have on it, and how is it reflected in the narratives themselves? These were central questions we wished to test.

As distinct from the past, the folklore researcher today does not regard himself as a person whose duty it is to salvage the folktale that is sentenced to extinction. We do not doubt that just as Moroccan Jews narrated folk narratives in their country of origin, so is a narrative tradition being generated in Israel. We regard the record we made in Shlomi, the record represented in this volume, as a photograph and documentation of the situation of the folk narrative of Moroccan Jews at a certain crossroads in time and space.

The study focused on two central elements: (a) textual research to examine the aesthetic qualities of the narrative, their division into genres, the various versions and their parallels, and acculturation in Israel; (b) contextual research to examine mainly the performance art of the narrator (intonation, gesticulation, mimics) and the location of the narrative as a communicative process in the narrating society. The collection comprises twenty-one narratives by twelve story-tellers, eleven were narrated by five women story-tellers, and ten were narrated by seven male story-tellers. Each narrative is accompanied by a commentary dealing with aspects we regard as most interesting and relevant, according to the points listed above.

Except for Rabbi Portal, who speaks Hebrew fluently and prefers presenting his narratives in Hebrew even for his family, the story-tellers perform their narratives in the Judeo-Arabic spoken by Moroccan Jews. This special dialect, spoken by this ethnic group, was used in conversing every day and also in composing their creations, both written and oral. The Judeo-Arabic language is interspersed with ancient Hebrew words used by Moroccan Jews, such as the names of holidays and rituals, which were pronounced with a special, typical intonation. We respected and encouraged the decision of the narrators to use their source language because we wanted to record the narratives as they are told in the community, not as told artificially at the request of a researcher. Interaction between the narrator, the audience, and the situation of performance forms the design of the folk narrative text; therefore, we attached the greatest importance to having local narrators addressing a local audience in their habitual language.

The fact that narrating in Judeo-Arabic is the usual way of narration of the community points to the place occupied by the ethnic culture of the group researched in Shlomi. Although they had resided in Israel for about twenty years when we recorded the narratives, the story-tellers still preferred to narrate in the source language. This is exclusively so in Shlomi; it is not representative of communities of this ethnic group settled in other locations throughout Israel, and it seems to us that the phenomenon is owing to two reasons: (a) we recorded the narratives from relatively old narrators (most of them were at least age sixty) some of whom were unable to acquire literary fluency in Hebrew (most can communicate in Hebrew in everyday situations, but a narrative requires a more idiomatic command than that); (b) the population of Shlomi was homogeneous, and the narrators were constantly surrounded by members of their own families with whom they generally lived. Hence the patterns of continuity were stronger than those we encountered elsewhere.[2]

An examination of the narratives, however, indicates that in addition to the ancient Hebrew words used by the story-tellers in their country of origin, the narratives also contain Hebrew words belonging to everyday language, words learned after immigration to Israel. This facet of the change points in the direction of future development.

As the stories were narrated in the source language, we are dealing with polished works of art using idioms, picturesque metaphors, and formulas. In the commentary appended to the narratives we have drawn the reader's attention to these qualities. We have pointed out such formulas as the typical opening "God was everywhere . . .," the closing formulas such as "The story flowed down with the rivers and we are left with generous givers," the sayings and the proverbs interwoven with the narratives, the tunes sung, and the euphemisms characteristic of the narrating society that assigns magic powers to the spoken word and therefore refrains from explicitly mentioning disastrous matters or takes care to add immediately that it dissociates itself from them or extends a blessing to the audience. For example, when the protagonist's mother in the narrative "Smeda Rmeda" dies, the narrator, Freḥa Ḥafutah, immediately turns to the audience and says: "The mother, she died, but may you not see trouble and bad things."

Our selections belong to three main genres: Various kinds of legends (47.6 percent), fairy tales (28.5 percent), novellas of subtlety and deceit of a humoristic nature (28.5 percent).[3] This division corresponds with the ethnic genre classification suggested by the narrators: *Ma'asseh, Hadīth* and *Kassiah.*

The importance of the ethnic categories was exhaustively discussed by Ben-Amos (1969, 1975), and we wanted to find out whether these categories exist in the ethnic tradition of Moroccan Jews. We established that the narrators refer to saint's legends as Ma'asseh, an archaic Hebrew word. It seems to us that the term

---

[2] Thus for instance, within the framework of a project in Beith-She'an we recorded from many Jewish Moroccan narrators who preferred narrating in Hebrew. For a discussion, see A. Shenhar and H. Bar-Itzhak, 1981; cf. Galit Hasan-Rokem, 1982, 129–137.

[3] The narrative "Never Trust the Dark-Haired Man" comprises two narratives, that belong to two different genres. This explains why the sum total is higher than 100 percent.

Shlomi.

Ma'asseh, as used by the narrators, derives from the meaning of the word in biblical literature where it refers to an action, to something being done. But mainly it is used by the narrators in the sense it was used by Ḥazal (the Sages), who consider the Ma'asseh as something anchored in a historic basis, containing a grain of fact and grounded in truth (Meir 1977, 4). Because these narratives are usually anchored in a geographical location and historical time, regarded as things the narrating society holds to be true, including supernatural occurrences, it is not surprising that they preserved the term Ma'asseh in its ancient sense to denote the genre of the legend.

As distinct from Ma'asseh, which derives from Jewish ancient sources, the term Ḥadīth was borrowed from the Arab environment where it equally denotes the genre of fairy tale.[4] The term Kassiah seems to derive from the Hebrew word *Kushiyah*. These realistic narratives are grounded in features of great subtlety or cunning of the protagonist that come out in situations where they have to solve a problem (Kushiyah), either verbally or through action.

Although we were able to establish ethnic categories for the genres, we would like to point out that this inquiry more so than any other highlighted the process of ongoing changes in the society. The elderly mostly tended to keep the genre terminology used in their country of origin, whereas younger people preferred the catego-

---

[4] The word *Ḥadīth* means primarily a communication or narrative in general.

ries used in Israel today. When we repeatedly questioned one narrator who used the classification accepted in Israel, she said: "In Morocco we called it differently, but my children studied stories like that at school, and that is why I know what these stories are really called." A society in an ongoing process of change, which has been uprooted and now lives in a different place, cannot be expected to use fixed and delimited ethnic genre terminology, but it is interesting to observe the process per se. The woman's remarks imply her preference for the terms used in Israel and her pride in her ability to use them. Moreover, she exemplifies the direction of the ongoing process of change that begins with the young generation and is passed on to the parents at a later stage.

The division into genres of the narratives narrated by men and women follows:

Narratives by women:[5]
    Fairy tales (54.5 percent)
    Legends (36.3 percent)
    Novellas of subtlety and deceit (18.1 percent)
Narratives by men:
    Legends (60 percent)
    Novellas of subtlety and deceit (40 percent)

The division establishes the relation to the various kinds of narratives by men and women. Men generally do not narrate fairy tales. This was moreover explicitly stated in our talks with narrators, who tended to dissociate themselves from this genre, regarding it as story-telling for women and children, not fit to be narrated by men. However, an investigation of all the narratives recorded by us in fieldwork (130 narratives) established that sometimes men also tell fairy tales. That is, no taboo is involved. We are dealing with a cultural preference that seems to derive from the fact that the fairy tale is a piece of fiction set in supernatural time and supernatural place where supernatural forces connected to the religious beliefs of the narrating society are not operative. Such stories apparently should not concern the Jewish Moroccan man.

As opposed to this, sacred legends and especially saint's legends are considered part of a holy genre. They discuss saints venerated by all Jews (Rabbi Abraham Iben Ezra in the present collection) or saints of an ethnic community (Rabbi Ḥaim Pinto and Rabbi Ḥaim Ben Atar in the present collection). They deal with holy religious values, with the Mitzvoth (commandments) between God and

---

[5] For the statistics see note 2.

Man and the Mitzvoth between Man and Man, and they are essentially didactic. This folk-religious genre of the narrating society is regarded as a legitimate genre by the men. The genre of the legend represents authority and hierarchy and metaphorically the place of men in Jewish-Moroccan society. In this society one duty performed by men is the formal transmission of values and behavioral norms.

The novellas are an expression of intellectual ability, and men like to narrate them because they contain elements of both subtlety and humor (see commentaries following the narratives). At the same time one should note that in the novellas narrated by men the clever character is always a man, whereas in the novellas narrated by women the picture is very different indeed.

The division into genres of women's stories shows that women like telling fairy tales. Some of these are very long, and they reflect worldly wisdom, though they chiefly give expression to the anxieties and secret wishes of feminine society. We have tried to treat this aspect more fully when commenting on the tales. As is well known, fairy tales do not deal with the world of religion, but because the narrators are religious women, the religious basis, absent on the level of plot, emerges on the linguistic level, in the opening and closing formulas and certain expressions woven into the narrative. For example, when the narrator points out that there was a big wedding she hastens to add "Nothing is great but only God," lest she might have uttered a blasphemy.

The women narrate both legends and novellas. That is to say, no folk genre is taboo to female society. As we mentioned above, in the novellas narrated by women the clever protagonists are women: Queen Alfahima, the Clever Girl. In these narratives a sexual confrontation takes place between a man and a woman, and the woman proves cleverer and more cunning than the man. In this way, expression is given to the wishes of the narrator and her listeners, but it would be wrong to regard these narratives as a challenge to the prevailing social order. We have dealt with this in the commentaries on the narratives.

At social gatherings it is customary for men to address a male audience and for women to address a female audience. For instance, men will narrate saint's legends in the yard of the synagogue, before and after prayers. But at family gatherings there is a mixed audience. The first narrator is a man, generally the head of the family. On one occasion a young man in his mid-twenties wanted us to come to his house to hear narratives from his mother. His father was at home, too. The mother prepared refreshments, and when all the members of the family were assembled in the family salon, the son asked his

19

The synagogue in Shlomi.

mother to narrate a story. The mother at once turned to her husband and asked him to do the narrating. When the head of the family had finished his narrative, the son again asked his mother to offer one of her narratives. Her reply was: "No, Father will narrate." Only after the same pattern of behavior had been repeated for the second time did the husband condescendingly admit her story-telling: "Alright, go ahead and tell your story." Then the wife agreed to start her narrative. This situation points to not only the narrating society's accepted patterns that date to the distant past but also the ongoing process of change that is given special expression by the son's behavior. He is undoubtedly familiar with the social and familial conventions, but he no longer accepts them.

The spiritual world underlying the narrative plots and determining the actions of the protagonists reflects the world of normative values of the narrating society—not only its world of beliefs and opinions, but also its tensions, anxieties, and wishes.

In the men's narratives the following points are stressed:

1. Religious confrontation between Jews and gentiles. Such confrontation occurs in 60 percent of the narratives. Noy pointed out that expressions of this confrontation are especially harsh and uncompromising in Jewish-Moroccan folk narratives (Noy 1974). The narratives in our selection also contain elements of contempt and humiliation. Two narratives illustrate this, "Who is Unclean?"

20

and "A Purim Miracle." Needless to say, the Jews invariably come out the winners, as the result of either a miracle (in sacred legends) or subtlety and cunning enabling them to outwit, or even to punish, the non-Jewish protagonist (in novellas of subtlety and deceit). In the commentaries we pointed out that many narratives of Jewish-gentile confrontation are structured like the Book of Esther; therefore, they restate this archetypal story about the struggle between Jews and gentiles in the Diaspora.

2. Confrontation between members of a family against an economic background. These narratives stress the importance of the commandments governing the relations between people and the importance of the family as a corporate body whose members must be loyal to one another.

3. Trust in God, observance of the Mitzvoth (commandments) between Man and God and between Man and Man. The commandments highlighted are holiday observance and Bible study.

Interestingly, only three narratives narrated by men feature woman characters, only one of whom is an active character. Depicted as extremely negative, she is rebuked in the strongest terms ("If God cares, he will punch a hole in the ceiling and pour down riches").

The women's narratives do not deal with any confrontations between Jews and gentiles. The women keep to intra-Jewish subjects and values, especially intrafamilial subjects. Those narrated by the two sexes focus on different areas because their societal functions differ: the men served as "ministers of the exterior" of the family, and contact with the outside world was their sole responsibility. The women raised the children and assumed responsibility within the framework of the family; however, their approach to the Muslim majority in their country of origin is projected on the linguistic level. For example, Freḥa Ḥafutah conveys her strong antagonism in the introductory formula: side by side with a blessing (addressed to the Jews) she curses the Muslims: "Our house is all silk and cotton, and may the house of the Muslims be destroyed and all of them be killed on one and the same day."

All the women's narratives feature female characters, and in the majority of narratives the woman is the protagonist (81.8 percent). How are the women depicted in their narratives? What are the most important traits of women? Patience and endurance predominate; also, the wife must be prepared to make even the supreme sacrifice if her husband requires it. This is shown in "The Patient Wife." The female protagonist of this narrative is prepared to sacri-

21

fice even her children for her husband's sake and to bear all the pain and suffering he causes her, without saying a word and without bitterness.

The woman is likewise expected to possess industry and foresight ("Never Trust the Dark Haired Man"); she must be her husband's obedient helpmate who trusts him and carries out his wishes even at the most critical times ("The story of Rabbi Ḥaim Pinto"). Other important qualities are love of her mother and distrust of strange women who try to intervene in the affairs of the family. Failure to possess these qualities is punishable (see "Smeda Rmeda," "Smeda Rmeda Who Turned into a Dove"). Acceptance of the spouse God has chosen for the woman is similarly important (for example, "What Is written in Heaven Cannot Be Wiped Out"). In addition to these features, the woman protagonists also possess wisdom and much cunning ("Queen Alfahima," "The Clever Girl"), the ability to protect their daughters ("My Sister Mass'uda and My Brother Mass'ud"), and the ability to secretly take the initiative to find a partner in marriage ("Smeda Rmeda," "Smeda Rmeda Who Turns into a Dove"). These features are regarded as positive and important in women. Nonetheless, it would be wrong to regard these narratives and the confrontations that end in the woman winning a victory over the man as narratives intended to overturn the existing social order. There certainly is an element of social protest and covert wishing; yet the clever woman who gets what she wants goes to the trouble of pacifying her husband, and to this end she calls him "the thing that is dearest to her." Again, the fact that she is required to be able to find a partner in marriage (by devious means) implies that she must learn to submit to male superiority and accept that her survival and honor depend on the husband and family who protect her. The narratives by women included in this selection reinforce the claim of feminist literature that argues women internalize the values and norms of the patriarchal society in which they were raised. As the women narrate their stories to young women who look up to them, there is an ongoing circular process of transmission of the values of patriarchal society by women to women.

Spiritually, the narratives reflect the Jewish-Moroccan worldview in their country of origin. What, then, is the basis for change following the encounter with Israeli culture? As shown above, first, the level of language has changed inasmuch as common everyday Hebrew words have found their way into the narratives. Also, the performance situation is undergoing a process of change. This is

Shlomi.

given expression by narrator Julliete Megera's testimony: interestingly, she reported that she mainly narrated when she was taking a bus ride, "to while away the time" and not in the evening, as was the custom in her country of origin because "everybody wants to watch television in the evening." It was also noted that genre terminology is changing, as the younger generation prefers the terminology used in Israel. Moreover, the realities of life in Israel are forcing their way into the narratives. New place names appear, and the new country supplies new metaphors and similes. When narrator Ḥaviva Dayan wishes to explain what distance the protagonist covered she says "like from Shlomi to Nahariya" (a town not far from Shlomi). In one narrative the husband wishes to describe a place he visited. He says to his wife: "He lives in some 'Moshav'" (communal Israeli village). Even the government of Israel, which pays a bonus to the parents of newborn babies, appears in the narratives—a new real-life situation. In connection with "The Stories of Mother Alaguz" we pointed out that the composition of the narrative gives expression to the wishes of the narrator following the encounter with realities of life in Israel that may deprive her of her position of dominance occupied in the old country.

The Shlomi narratives reflect the old world and express patterns of continuity rather than patterns of change. Nevertheless, changes occur and are noticeable. In every ethnic group there are ongoing processes of segregation along with processes of integration (Katzir 1982, 264–273). Our narratives are a documentation of the situation of the folk narrative of Moroccan Jews at a certain crossroads in time and space.

23

## INTRODUCTION

We take pleasure in thanking all those who assisted with the publication of this book, the Israel Folktale Archives, the Lucius N. Littauer Foundation and the Faculty of the Humanities of the University of Haifa. We are especially indebted to Raphael Patai who unsparingly gave us of his time and valuable counsel and to Dan Ben-Amos for his encouragement and excellent suggestions for improving the manuscript. We also thank Edna Cheichel who read the manuscript with incisive thoroughness and to Riva Friedman for meticulous proofreading. Arthur B. Evans has made our association with Wayne State University Press a particularly happy one, and in Lynn H. Trease we have found an exemplary editor. We owe a special debt of gratitude to Zeev Bar-Itzhak for his enormous help with the technical preparation of the manuscript.

# Ḥaviva Dayan

Ḥaviva Dayan was about ninety years old when the narratives were recorded. She came from Marakesh, Morocco, where her parents, David and Sa'ada, lived. In 1954, she and her family came to Israel, where her mother died at the age of ninety. At first, they settled in Massoa, which is next to Hartuv; then they moved to Noam, and they finally settled in Shlomi in 1965. When we recorded her narratives, she was living with her son Asher and his family.

Her husband died forty-three years ago, when her youngest daughter was three months old. He left her some money to live on, but she had to work at all kinds of jobs to provide for her family. Of the thirteen children she bore, only three were alive when we recorded her narratives. She regarded her daughter's death as especially tragic because she died soon after her son was born. The daughter, who was the mother of five daughters, had wanted a son. Soon after the mother's death, the son died, too. When Ḥaviva spoke of her daughter, she stressed that she was a pious woman who observed the laws of ritual purification most carefully.

In Morocco, Ḥaviva did sewing, and in Shlomi she stitches colorful cushions using left-over pieces of material.

25

In her childhood, Ḥaviva would listen to the folk narratives by members of her family on different occasions during the day and on ritual occasions such as Brith Milah (circumcision) and the guarding of the women after giving birth.

She no longer has the opportunity to listen to folk narratives, but she still narrates to the members of her family on different occasions during the day and especially on Sabbath. According to her testimony, family members like to listen to her narratives.

# The Patient Wife

FROM: ḤAVIVA DAYAN

Let me tell you, God was everywhere. Until there was a rich man.[1] Come to this rich merchants' house and see for yourself: he did not beget any children. He would fast, distribute money, write amulets, and visit the tombs of saints, until finally one daughter was born to him. She would say to the sun: "Shine, or I will shine on God our Maker who created both you and me." In beauty and stature, in her whiteness and crimson she was the image of perfection.

The daughter grew up. Whenever someone asked for her hand in marriage, the father would say: "He who does not give me three kuntars[2] of goods cannot marry my daughter."

They said to him: "What are the three kuntars for?"

He said to them: "One for her beauty, one for the hair she virtually walks upon, and one for her patience."

One man rose and said: "Her beauty—we see that she is very beautiful; her hair—we see that no other girl has her hair; but patience—what if she is not patient?

He said to them: "You try her out for a year. If, at the end of

---

[1] This is the typical opening of the Jewish Moroccan folktale. It invites the audience to listen, stresses the importance of the element of holiness embedded in the tale, and focuses attention on the story that is going to unfold. Up to the events covered by the story, God was everywhere, but following the opening the protagonist of the story claims our attention.

[2] Unit of weight also used in Israel; the equivalent of 288 kg, or 256 kg in Syria.

this period, you find that she is not patient, I shall return the kuntar you gave me for her patience."

All the young men in the town asked for her hand in marriage, but none could raise three kuntars of goods, the poor creatures.

One day, as they were all sitting in the coffee-house and playing games, the girl went by; she was going to the bath-house.

Now a wealthy merchant from another town arrived in the town. He came with two suitcases full of money and wanted to have a good time. He saw the young men sitting in front of the coffee-house. He asked them: "What are you doing?"

They said to him: "We are playing cards, or checkers, or other games."

He sat down with them. He said to them: "Have you paid for the coffee you are having? If not, I will pay."

What did it matter to them?[3]

They said to him: "The coffee has already been paid for, but if you want to stand us another round, do so—why not?"

They brought them the cups of coffee, and as they were drinking the man raised his eyes and saw the girl who was returning from the bath-house. She radiated beauty. The instant he saw her he froze in his seat, as if stung.

He said to them: "Are you single or are you married?"

They said to him: "We are single."

He said to them: "You have this superb beauty of a girl in your midst—not married, not engaged?"

They said to him: "Not married, not engaged, and still a virgin."

He said to them: "Are you dead, or are you alive? You have this beautiful girl in your midst, and you don't get married?"

They said: "Her father won't let us. He demands three kuntars, and we do not have that kind of money. Everybody in this town has asked for her hand in marriage, but he will not give her to anyone, seeing that nobody has three kuntars."

He said to them: "I will give him six kuntars so I can marry her tonight. If he does not agree I will die." (He sees so beautiful a girl—and she does not belong to anyone.)[4]

They said to him: "Good, let us call the matchmaker."[5]

They went and called the matchmaker.

---

[3] With the words, said in Hebrew, the story-teller interrupts her own narrative and offers her opinion of the events.

[4] The narrator's aside.

[5] Literally, "The person who asks for [the] hands [of girls in marriage]."

He said to him: "Go and ask for the hand of this girl in marriage."

He said to him: "Brother, I will not go and ask for her hand in marriage. Her father warned me, saying: 'Anyone who does not bring me three kuntars of goods—even if he says he has them and will give them to you, do not come to me. If you do not bring the goods, don't you ever come here.'"

He said to him: "I will give him four kuntars as long as you go and ask for her hand in marriage."

He said to her father: "A Jew who lives in another city is in town. He has lots of money, he is a rich man."

He said to him: "Will he give me three kuntars worth of goods?"

He said: "He will."

The young man said: "What are the three kuntars for?"

He said to him: "One kuntar for her beauty, one kuntar for her hair, and one kuntar for patience."

He said to him: "Good. But let us make a deal: I will give you the money I carry in my suitcases. For the balance, I will go back to my town. I will transfer my business to this city, I will buy a store and a home, and I will live here. And the wedding will be in two weeks."

He said to him: "Go."

He went back to the town where he lived. He sold everything. He sold expensive things for little money, he brought money, he brought furniture, he brought a bus, he kept bringing things.

Good. He married the girl, there was a big wedding—none but God is great.

Good, when he married her—when he looked at her, he saw a hundred faces. She would dress up, and they would go out together.

She became pregnant; she had a boy. The child was one year old; when he was in his second year, she was sitting at home when her husband came home from the store. He knocks on the door.

She said to him: "Who is it?"

He said to her: "Open the door, open the door, open the door, I am going to die. The pain that started when I was in the store is going to kill me."

—"I am your substitute, I am your compensation, I am your redemption.[6] Whatever is to happen to you, let it happen to me."

---

[6] Was said in Hebrew "Ani kapparatkha, ani halifatkha, ani temuratkha," a quotation from the Kapparot ritual on the Day of Atonement.

She opened the door; he entered.

She said to him: "But why do you come here? why do you come to me? Go and see a doctor. Do you want me to go to the doctor with you?"

He said to her: "No, no. Don't go to the doctor with me."

He left. For half an hour he sat with his friends, plays, laughs, and feels happy. Then he went back home.

She said to him: "Did you go to the doctor?"

He said to her: "I did."

She said to him: "And what did he tell you?"

—"He told me that if I have a son or a daughter I must slaughter him and drink his blood and smear his blood on my body in order to get well."

She said to him: "He is turned about and sacrificed instead of you."[7]

She took the child she had borne, who was by now two years old, washed him, dressed him, kissed him, and gave him to his father.

He took the child. Where did he take him? Let us say to a place as far away from his home as is Nahariya from Shlomi, to a teacher who instructs the children of the wealthy. He called her and said: "My daughter, you take care of this child, and I will pay all your expenses. Give him the food the rich eat, and dress him the way the rich dress, and I will pay for everything."

He went to his store, washed his face and hands, and went home.

She said to him: "Well, what happened?"

He said to her: "Good, my daughter. I felt a little better, and I dropped in on my friends. I did not want to come home with blood all over me."

She said to him: "And what did the doctor tell you?"

He said to her: "What did he tell me? He said I should sleep for half an hour, have lunch, and go for a ride in a taxi cab in the evening."

They ate, and they drank. Her servant, who had been a servant in her father's house, and who had been given her by her father as a gift, helped her. She dressed, she washed, she put on makeup, and they went for a ride in the car, till eight o'clock in the evening.

---

[7] The words "turned about and sacrificed instead of you" are a quotation from the Kapparot ritual (the sacrifice of the cock) on the Day of Atonement. They imply that the boy will lay down his life for his father.

Good, she became pregnant again. Pregnant for nine months, three months—on heat, three—getting fat, and three—she clutches the rope.[8] "He who saves from trouble, may He save her."

She had another baby, a boy even more beautiful than her first child.

Good, she was happy: she dresses him, she gives him food, she gives him drink, she takes him for a walk—until he is two years old.

He is two years and one day old, and again she is at home when suddenly her husband arrives. He knocks on the door.

She said: "Who is it?"

He said to her: "Open the door, open the door, open the door, I am in pain. The pain is going to kill me."

—"I am your substitute, I am your compensation, I am your redemption."

He enters the room.

She said to him: "Why did you come to me? Go to the doctor. Do you want me to go with you?"

He said to her: "No, no, don't come with me. Don't tire yourself. I will go by myself."

He left, sat in his store, plays, laughs with his friends, plays checkers until half an hour has passed. Then he went back home.

She said to him: "What did he tell you?"

He said to her: "My daughter, what was he to tell me? He said: 'What you did the first time, you must do the second time. If you have a son or a daughter, slaughter him, smear his blood on your body, and you will recover.'"

She said to him: "He is turned about and he is sacrificed, so you stay alive."

She took the second child, washed him, dressed him, kissed him, and handed him to her husband.

He took the child to his brother.

He said to the woman: "My daughter, I brought you the first child when he was two years old, and now he is four. Take him to the big school, and teach the second boy at home, and I will pay all your expenses. Buy them blankets, and cook rich men's food for them, and buy rich men's clothes for them, and raise them the way the rich raise their children. And be forebearing, and do not tell them they are brothers. They must grow up without knowing they are brothers."

Good, she did so.

Good, the wife became pregnant again. Three—in heat,

---

[8] Women used to hold a rope in their hands during parturition.

three—getting fat, three—she clutches the rope. "He who saves from trouble, may He save her from trouble."

She bore a daughter—more beautiful than her mother.

She loves this daughter, and she says: "To-morrow is the Ninth Day of the Month of Ab."[9]

She dressed her, she washed her, she took her for walks, until she was two years old.

She was two years old, and again, one day she is at home, and her husband arrives and knocks.

She said: "Who is it?"

He said: "Open the door. This time it is worse than it was the first time and the second time. This time I nearly died on my way home."

—"I am your substitute, I am your compensation, I am your redemption."

She said to him: "Why did not you go to the doctor?"

He said to her: "I was afraid to go, lest he might say what he said before."

She said to him: "You must go. Whatever he says, do it. If he says you must slaughter me too and drink my blood to get well, I will give you my blood."

He left. Again, he joined his friends, plays games, laughs, talks to people in his store, until half an hour had gone by. He returned home.

She said to him: "What did he tell you?"

—"What should I tell you, my daughter? He said if I have a son or a daughter I must slaughter him, drink his blood, and rub my body with it. Then I will get well."

She said to him: "She is turned about, she is sacrificed instead of you—as long as you stay alive."

She washed her, dressed her, the poor woman, she gave her two kisses, and handed her to him.

He took her to the house where her brothers were living. He said to the schoolteacher: "Of all my children this child is dearest to me." He called the schoolteacher aside, so the boys should not overhear their conversation. He said to her: "The first boy is six, the second is four, and the girl is two. Whatever money you spend to raise them, I will pay you back."

Good. He kissed his boys, and he kissed his daughter.

—"Do not tell them that she is their sister, and do not tell

---

[9] She mourns, fearing for her daughter's life. The ninth Day of Ab is the day of the destruction of the Temple.

them that they are brothers. Let them grow up without their knowing it."

Good, he returned home. She served him some food, they had a meal, they went to sleep, they took a shower, and went for a bus ride till eight o'clock. They returned home.

Good, years went by. The child grew up, and the first-born turned thirteen.

One day the husband did not come home to have his midday meal; he came back in the evening and brought his wife a bag of cookies.

She said to him: "Where have you been? Why didn't you come home for your midday meal?"

He said to her: "Someone I know invited me to attend his son's Bar-Mitzvah.[10] I went to his house, and I gave that poor, penniless man some money."

She said to him: "Why did you not take me with you?"

He said to her: "Why should I take you there? The place is a wasteland. He lives in a Moshav[11] that is not nice. I am a man, but you, you would not have anyone to sit with when you go there. Who would you talk to, the Arab women? Or the Jewish women?"

He gave her the bag of cookies. And he made a Bar-Mitzvah for his eldest son, his firstborn.

Time went by. Then the second son turned thirteen. His father made a Bar-Mitzvah for him. Again, he did not come home for his midday meal. She said to him: "Where have you been?"

He said to her: "Somebody's son was having his Bar-Mitzvah, and the poor father had no money. I gave him some, and he gave me these cookies, and he said: 'Give them to your wife, I want her to taste them.'"

Good, years went by. The boy grew up; the girl was seventeen (in tales, girls grow up fast). She was seventeen, and her father sees that she is even more beautiful than her mother.

He said to his wife: "My daughter, you mean a great deal to me, and I must tell you something, but don't get angry."

She said to him: "I will not get angry, no matter what you say."

He said to her: "God took the children we had, and I long for children. I am so rich, and if I die tomorrow, there will be no heirs to whom I can leave my money and my possessions."

---

[10] A ceremony that marks the transition from childhood to adulthood in Jewish society.

[11] Communal Israeli village.

She said to him: "I will be happy to find you a wife, and I will give her to you in marriage, and I myself will arrange the wedding. As soon as you show me the girl you want, I will arrange the marriage."

He said to her: "I will take you to the door of the house where she lives, but I will not come in. I will take you to the door, and you will see a girl and her teacher enter the house (his daughter!)[12] That is the girl I want. Tell her that you want her for a man you know, a very wealthy man, and that she need not give you any money or anything else. Take her away, with only her clothes on her back." He pointed out the house to her. She went there, and she entered. She saw her, she had adorned herself with gold, and the beauty God had given her had diminished. The teacher greeted her and kissed her: "Welcome, welcome, welcome. What is it you want? Why are you so unhappy? What made you come here today?"

She said to her: "My daughter, they tell me you have a beautiful daughter. Give her to me; I want her for a man with whom we are acquainted and who is wealthy. You do not have to provide her with clothes or with anything else. We will take her naked."

She said to her: "I wish your worries were my worries. I will give her to you even if she is going to be no more than a servant. He does not have to make her his wife."

She said to her: "They are going to get married this week. I will get someone to perform the wedding ceremony."

Good. She went to different places; she had the house whitewashed, she did the sewing, she shined the pots and pans, she did not leave anything undone. There was not a thing she did not do. She got everything ready for the bridal night.

Good. The girl arrived.

He bathed; he got dressed. They brought her in; she was wearing a bridal veil and a white dress. They made her stand beside him.

A woman who was holding a candle stood behind the rich man's wife, and there! Some of her hair caught fire.

She said to her: "Wife of the rich man, wife of the rich man, your hair has caught fire, your hair is on fire."

She said to her: "It is not my hair that is on fire. My heart is on fire."

She had uttered these words when the husband jumped off the table and took her, put her on his shoulders and started whirling

---

[12] Narrator's aside, to heighten the tension.

33

Ketuba, a marriage contract, Tatuan, M. Kaniel collections. By kind permission of the Israel Museum, Jerusalem.

round the room and dancing, whirling around the room and dancing, whirling around the room and dancing.

He said to them: "Where is my father-in-law who demanded one kuntar for her patience? Go and find him."

When he arrived, he said to him: "Now I will pay you another six kuntars. Where has there ever been a woman who would not weep, would not shed tears when her three children were taken from her? And who would say 'Let them be turned around and sacrificed in your stead,' so they give their lives for me? Good, come here, my daughter, here are your two sons. The first bag of cookies I brought

34

you was from the Bar-Mitzvah of your eldest boy, and the second bag I brought you was from the Bar-Mitzvah of your younger son. And this is your daughter. And now call the rabbi who wanted to marry us."

They called him.

He said to him: "Rabbi, I ask God and you to bring me the youth who is the best student and the most good-looking. Even if he does not have a penny to his name—if he is bright and handsome, bring him."

They brought him.

He had a suit made for him; they made him wear the suit, and he married the girl. He took his wife and went to his house and the people applauded him.

Good. He said to them: "Now, you people of Ḥallaba,[13] who won? Is not this true patience? What woman would let go of her three children and say: 'Let them be turned around and sacrificed instead of you, and if you want to slaughter me too, do it.' Can anyone be more patient than that? Which woman would ever do such a thing?"

Good, he took her away, and they lived like newlyweds; they loved each other, and they had fun together.

His daughter married a rabbi. Her father bought her a house, he bought her furniture, and bought her everything.

And his children—he sent them to university and paid the tuition fee.

And the tale floats on the rivers,
And you, my friends, are generous givers.

## Commentary: IFA 16433

### THE PATIENT WIFE

This tale belongs to the type named after Griselda, the long-suffering and patient wife (Aarne-Thompson 887).

In the Middle Ages, this type was widespread in Europe[1] and the Middle East.[2] Parallel narratives preserved in the Israel Folktale

---

[13] It may be assumed that the narrator does not refer to a specific place and uses this name for a legendary place.

[1] Cf. Siefkin 1903; Laserstein 1926.

[2] Cf. Eberhard and Boratav 1953; Dawkins 1953.

Archives (IFA) are essentially Middle Eastern[3]—a woman's test of endurance (Motif H 461). According to these narratives, the perfect wife is willing to suffer, to give up everything, and to sacrifice even her children to please her husband.

We learn from the testimony of the narrator that the tale was widely spread in Morocco. She first heard it from a friend who told it at a mixed social gathering of both women and men, and then she heard it repeatedly at similar gatherings. Ḥaviva Dayan narrates it in her own home, and not only on special occasions; she usually narrates it several times each year.

The fact that the narrative is presented to a mixed group and that the narrator may be either a man and or a woman indicates to what extent the women have internalized the values and norms of a patriarchal society.

The tale certainly deals with a confrontation between the sexes; the narrator identifies completely with the suffering wife, but it equally expresses female pride in women's power of endurance. There is not a single word of condemnation of the way the husband puts his wife to the test, even though the sheer horror of it is made very clear.

The manner in which the events are presented implies criticism of the husband, but disapproval is not conveyed in order to bring about behavioral change because the husband's conduct is felt to be consonant with the essence of the male psyche: when the husband appears for the second time and tells his wife that he is in great pain, both the audience and the wife know what is going to happen because the earlier test called for the slaughter of the eldest son. In the manner of the folk narrative we are not told what the wife felt when her husband was away, but listeners fill in this gap by themselves, and hence the behavior of the husband, who plays games with his friends, tends to elicit a negative response on their part.

The seriousness of the situation is restated with greater intensity when the husband pays the third visit. The effect is achieved by two devices, repetition and contrast. The visit is repeated three times over, and the behavior of the wife is contrasted with that of the husband. The wife says: "Just go to the doctor, and whatever he tells you—do it. If he tells you to slaughter me and drink my blood, I will give it to you," but the husband sits with his friends and laughs and plays games.

However, the tale does not intend to change the male pattern

---

[3] From Tunis (2), published in Noy 1966, no. 31; Noy 1967, no. 1. Israel Sefardi (1), Samaritans (1).

of behavior, and although condemnation is implied, the husband's behavior is felt to be consonant with the male essence; somehow, men have the right to put their wives to the test even if it involves the most terrible of ordeals.

The full extent of the test's horror is reflected in the store of images upon which the woman draws. Certain phrases associated with the Day of Atonement recur over and over again. The words "My life is your substitute, my life is your compensation, my life is your redemption" accompany the ritual of expiation traditionally performed on the Eve of the Day of Atonement, and the words "And it is turned around and sacrificed in your stead" refer to the slaughter of a cock that substitutes for a human life.

Equally, fear of what the future may have in store for the daughter is conveyed by the words: "Tomorrow is the Ninth Day of the Month of Ab."

Lastly, the woman's reply "It is not my hair that has caught fire. It is my heart," concretizes the wife's feelings that, in the manner of the folktale, are not described.

The intensity of the husband's feelings, too, is conveyed through his actions: when he realizes the full extent of the woman's powers of endurance as she passes the last test, he "got off the table, took her and placed her on his shoulders and started turning round and dancing, turning round and dancing, turning round and dancing."

Incidentally, in the international type the king marries a socially inferior girl, and she promises she will forever be content with her lot; here, too, he lets her prove this by staging the killing of her children and making another woman his wife. The king-husband thus takes advantage of the wife's inferior social status to put her to the test and subject her to severe trials, and it appears that socially inferior women are superior when put to the test, in the manner of "a topsy-turvy world," a motif popular with folk narrators.[4]

Our version, however, does not polarize differences of class. Instead, there is the latent confrontation between father and daughter. This comes out into the open on rare occasions only: the father makes excessive demands on his daughter's suitors, which affects her married life later on. The facts that the father had been childless and that his daughter was born only after a lengthy period of prayer, alms giving, and so on contribute to the father-daughter relation-

---

[4] Cf., e.g., the narrative type "Betting on the fidelity of the wife." Aarne-Thompson 882 (Noy 1973, note to no. 3).

ship. The opening of the story implies how much the daughter meant to her father, even though his love for her is never verbalized. Yet he raises difficulties when suitors ask for her hand in marriage, and she does not rebel.

Perhaps a comparison of the various versions of this narrative brings out the "male" causes underlying the father's relationship with his daughter and the nature of the confrontation between father and daughter, which is basically sexual. This assumption is further substantiated by the fact that the mother does not have any part in the plot.

The daughter, who does not rebel against her father, equally does not rebel against her husband, which shows that an obedient daughter is an obedient wife. Her removal from the sphere of authority of the father to that of the husband is not what she had wished for, and yet she passes the test. This message is a feature of this type of tale of endurance that instructs the listeners to steel themselves, for it tells women that life, with all it has in store for men, is nothing but a test that women are able to pass.

Perhaps the words "Shine, or else I will shine on God who has created both you and me," which the girl directs to the sun, signify arrogance, self-assurance, self-praise; their impact may well surface as the story progresses. The girl takes pride in her beauty, and pride is a sin that needs to be punished. Actually, we might say that the girl failed when God, who gives human beings beauty, put her humility to the test; conversely, she succeeded when her husband tested her patience. Perhaps this further justifies the actions of the husband, although normative Jewish religion leaves punishment in God's hands. Consequently, justification of the cruel behavior of the husband is also embedded in the plot.

As we pointed out above, the girl wins a victory in the confrontation between her and her husband: she committed the sin of pride when she spoke (she addressed the sun), but she made up for the wrong she had committed when she exercised self-restraint and did not speak.

The narrative employs the device of a dramatic situation: the listeners know more than one of the characters: they know that the children have not died. Consequently, their curiosity is aroused, and they want to learn how this character (the wife) discovers the truth and what her reaction is going to be. But when the husband asks his wife to give him his daughter in marriage, the audience is beginning to doubt the future development, and they suspect that perhaps this is not part of the test; the man who broke a taboo—he claimed he murdered his children and drank their blood—is really going to break a taboo now. Hence the audience is relieved when it discovers that this is just another part of the test, which moreover ends well, in keeping with the norms of society. The dance that the husband performs expresses the listeners' joy when the familiar and right order of things is restored.

The fact that the listeners identify with this tale proves that they agree with the truths it conveys. The tale, handed down from one generation to the next, is felt to be worth listening to.

The tale contrasts the qualities of the soul with those of the body. The girl has three qualities: beauty, long hair, and patience. In return for these qualities the father demands three kuntars. The bridegroom questions the father about the third invisible quality, but it is most important to him and allows the plot to unfold. By the time this quality is revealed the wife no longer possesses the two others: her beauty has faded, and her hair has been burnt off; but this does not prevent her husband from loving her even more than before. The spiritual quality is therefore the most essential. This emerges when the husband offers to pay his father-in-law another, larger sum of money: "Now I will pay you an additional six kuntars."

We should also note the narrator's art. The opening and the conclusion of the tale are typical of the Moroccan folktale. The opening invites the assembled guests to listen, stresses the element of holiness, and draws the listeners' attention to the events to be narrated. The conclusion underlines the element of fiction—"and the tale floats on the rivers"—and does honor to the listeners—"and my friends, are generous givers."

The narrator uses certain idioms that she interweaves with the tale: "Three months in heat, three months getting fat, three months—she clutches the rope, oh He who saves [people] from troubles, save her from her troubles."

It is, moreover, interesting to note how the narrator links the past to the present. On the one hand, we have a description of the traditional way of life, with men sitting in a coffee-house, drinking coffee, playing games, and watching the passersby, or a man sitting in his shop with his wife staying at home and raising the children. On the other hand, life in Israel today surfaces. For example, the narrator refers to a trip from Shlomi, where she currently resides, to Nahariya so the listeners can picture to themselves the distance covered by the protagonist, and the nurse in the tale is an Israeli elementary school teacher; also, she mentions a settlement in Israel, a taxi cab, and a bus. The present is contained in the past—tangible proof of the vital strength of the folktale.

# The Tales of Mother Alaguz

FROM: HAVIVA DAYAN

The day Mother Alaguz was born,[1] a penny appeared in her hand. A penny of those days. She clutched it in her hand, like that, when she came out of her mother's belly. Alongside the penny there was a note saying that the penny would support her for life.

Days went by, and days came, on and on. Mother Alaguz grew up and got married. Mother Alaguz got old. Mother Alaguz became an old woman. Whenever she offered her penny to somebody and said: "Give me vegetables for this penny," they would say: "Go, mother Alaguz! Take that penny of yours, what is a penny worth? Go, take your penny," and they would give her vegetables.

She would go to the butcher and say to him: "Give me meat for this penny," and he would say to her: "Mother Alaguz, this penny is worthless. Take the meat and go away, and take your penny."

Over and over again, over and over again. All those she went to told her the same thing.

One day she went out and bought a bundle of fish. As she was carrying the fish, there arose a storm, a storm and rain. She wrapped her head in a sheet. When she tried to raise her eyes she found herself at the entrance to the king's house, and around it guards are standing.

She said: "Now what is this? Where did this storm take me?"

They said to her: "This is the king's house."

She said to them: "What is this?"

The guard who was there said to her: "Oh, Mother Alaguz, why did you come now, in this storm, in these winds?"

She said to him: "Consult with the king on my behalf, and if he allows me to come in, I will get through the night and be fine, and if he does not allow me to come in, I will sit down here and I will die."

He went and told all this to the king.

---

[1] According to our informants, Alaguz is a term used in Judeo-Arabic language when referring to an old woman.

The king said to him: "Go and bring this Mother Alaguz. . . . Old women are good, and they say sweet things. Go and bring her to amuse us a little."

Good, she entered. She kissed his hand, and she kissed his head. She sat down.

—"Mother Alaguz, would you like something to eat, would you like something to drink?"

She said to him: "I will eat, and I will drink."

They brought her the food; they brought her the drink. When she came in, she found the king's wife standing. The king's wife snatched the bundle of fishes she was holding in her hand and swallowed them. His wife was a demon. She swallowed the fish, with the bones and with the innards.

Mother Alaguz said: "Woe! Now eat me for dessert! I will go to the king."

She went to the king. The king's wife came, poured them tea, brought them supper; they ate and drank.

The king said to her: "Tell me a story."

She said to him: "Till you finish your supper I will tell you the story, and dance and sing to you."

When the king had finished his supper, his wife brought him a cup with a sleeping draught. He drank it. When Mother Alaguz saw that he was asleep she too wrapped herself in her sheet and left a small chink in her sheet. Through the chink she watched the king's wife, to see what she was doing. The king's wife left. She left, and Mother Alaguz rose and followed her, slowly, slowly, slowly, to the back of the house. The she-demon called her mother: "Oh mother! Oh mother!"

She answered her: "Yes."

She said to her: "Let me, Mother, eat supper, or I will eat you and the king!"

—"Go, you madwoman. You will eat me and the king for supper?!"

She said to her: "Go and get me some supper, or else I will sup on you and the king!"

She said to her: "Go, here are two mules. Their owner has brought them a short time ago. Go see them in the stable and eat them for supper, and I will pay the owner tomorrow morning."

She went there, and Mother Alaguz watches her all the time.

She went there and entered this stable. She stretched out her hand and tore the innards out of the belly of one of the animals, stretched out her hand again and tore out the innards of the other animal, and sat down. She eats and tears [the innards] to pieces

41

again, and again, and again, and again, and again. She started eating their flesh, and they bray.

And Mother Alaguz watches all this—until she finished.

When she licked the bones, Mother Alaguz left, wrapped herself up, and fell asleep.

The woman—when she was finished she went to the shower, washed, changed her clothes, and went to sleep beside the king.

Good, dawn broke. The she-demon brought the king a cupful of drink to counteract the effect of the sleeping draught.

She said to him: "My lord, drink this cup of cold water so you recover and get up."

The king drank, got up, and wandered about in his house. The woman went and brought tea, and brought milk, and brought all she brought. They ate and drank, and the king left.

At night, the king said to Mother Alaguz again: "Oh Mother Alaguz, you did not tell us anything yesterday."

She said to him: "Oh my Lord, what shall I tell you? You had supper, and you fell asleep. Perhaps you want me to tell the walls something? Stay awake, and I will tell you stories, and sing and dance for you."

And she did not want to tell him about all she had seen in connection with his wife.

Again the she-demon brought them supper. They finished their supper, and she gave him the same cup again. He drank it and fell asleep. When Mother Alaguz saw him like that, she covered herself with her little sheet and left the same chink open to peep through and watch.

The she-demon said: "They are all asleep." She went, opened the house and stepped outside. And Mother Alaguz followed her. She walks, and she follows her. She came to her mother: "Oh mother! Oh mother!

She said to her: "Yes."

She said to her: "Give me some supper, or I will eat you and the king."

—"Go, you madwoman, oh you madwoman! Oh you crazy woman. People pay millions to see the king, and you want to eat him for supper?"

She said to her: "If that is so, give me something for supper because I am hungry. Tonight I am hungry."

She said to her: "Go, there is a pair of camels. Their owner brought them here. Eat them for supper, and tomorrow I will pay for them."

She entered the stable and found those two camels. She stretched out her hand and tore out their innards and ate them. Mother Alaguz stood and watched. When she had finished the innards she started tearing off their flesh, and they brayed with pain. And so on, until she finished eating. When she was licking the bones, Mother Alaguz returned and fell asleep. The she-demon returned, went to the shower, washed, put on a new dress, and went to sleep beside the king.

The next morning, she brought him the cupful of drink again in order to wake him. He woke, recovered, and walked about and observed. The woman went downstairs to get the milk, the coffee, everything. Mother Alaguz said: "Oh my Lord."

He said to her: "Yes."

She said to him: "You are married to a she-demon."

—"What did you say, oh Mother Alaguz?!"

She said to him: "You are married to a she-demon. If she is not a she-demon, kill me."

He said to her: "And how do you know that?"

She said to him: "Now I will not tell you anything. I will stay with you until nightfall, and then you can go with me and see everything. But there is one thing you must do."

He said to her: "What is that?"

She said to him: "When you finish your supper and she serves you a cup of tea, put a towel on your lap, and when she hands you the cup of tea, pour it onto the towel and keep quiet. Even if she shakes you, do not move."

Good. The woman went and brought them coffee, brought them tea; they drank; they ate; they drank.

The she-demon said to Mother Alaguz: "Mother Alaguz, come, come down, I want to tidy up the house."

The king went to his government house. They cooked dinner and ate.

The she-demon cooked supper and carried it to the king. He ate. Again, she brought him the same cup. He put the towel on his lap, emptied the content of the cup into the towel, and kept quiet. The she-devil returned, shook him, and he did not move. Mother Alaguz peeped through the chink in the sheet, pretended she was asleep, and said neither yes nor no.

The she-demon left again. She went down, down, down, down, until she got there.

—"Oh my mother! Oh my mother!"

She said to her: "Yes."

She said to her: "Get me some supper, or else I will sup on you and the king."

—"Go, oh you madwoman. Sup on the king?! People pay millions to see him, and you want to eat him!?"

She said to her: "Tonight I am hungry, get me something to eat."

She said to her: "Go, there are two donkeys. Their owner brought them here and put them in the stable. Eat them, and tomorrow I will pay the owner."

She went where these donkeys were. And the king stands there and watches. He and Mother Alaguz. When the she-demon left, Mother Alaguz rose and said to him: "My lord."

He said to her: "Yes."

She said to him: "Rise, come with me to see your wife."

He went with her. He stood there, looked, and trembled all over.

He said to her: "Oh Mother Alaguz, this [creature] will not let go until she finishes me. And now, what am I to do?"

She said to him: "What you are going to do? Tomorrow at first light take a hundred guards with you. They must dig a well for you, and they must not throw away the earth, but leave it beside the well. And put up a tent over the well, and slaughter a sheep and call people, and call musicians and call singers. When they come, call your wife and tell her: 'Put on your gold [ornaments], and put on your dress and go and watch the musicians and the games.' And you cover the well with a carpet and place a small chair on it. When she comes, tell her: 'Come and have a look at the tent, you have never seen it before.' When she comes and sits down, she will fall into the well, and that is what is going to save you. If that does not save you, nothing will save you."

He went, the way it has been told, and did so. He sent the guards and slaughtered the sheep. They got the pots ready and prepared kuskus.[2] They dug the well, put the carpet across the well, and put up the tent.

So the people ate and drank, and they left. Only the king and his wives stayed behind, and Mother Alaguz and the servant girls.

When his wife was leaving, the king said to her: "Come and have a look at this tent, you have never seen such [a tent] before." She entered.

---

[2] A traditional Moroccan dish prepared with semolina. For more details on kuskus dishes, see p. 101.

He said to her: "Sit on this small chair."

She sat on the chair and fell into the pit.

The she-demon cried: "Oh king, this is treachery! Oh king, this is treachery!"

And he did not answer her.

The guards came. They shoveled the earth back into the pit, more, and more, until the pit was filled.

They went home. Mother Alaguz said: "Oh my lord, I wish to leave."

He said to her: "Oh Mother Alaguz, sleep and stay until the next day, and I will give you a saddle-bag of flour, a saddle-bag of sugar, I will give you oil, I will give you salted butter, I will give you . . ."

She said to him: "I will not take anything. I will not take anything from you except my little penny. I brought it here, in my hand, and I dropped it. Return it to me."

The king said to her: "Oh Mother Alaguz, sleep over, and I will command [the servants] to cut sheets for you, and I will give you a warm dress, I will give you . . . I will give you . . ."

She said to him: "I have everything."

So he kissed her hand and her head and said to her: "This is in return for saving me and for what you have done for me."

He gave her her little penny, and she went away, away, away, away.

Again there came rain and stormy winds, stormy winds. She put her kerchief on her head, and she did not know where she was going.

On, and on, and on, till nightfall. Again she found herself at the entrance to the house of a king. The guards rose and said to her: "Mother Alaguz, what made you come here at such a time?"

She said to them: "The stormy winds brought me here, the wind brought me, and now go and speak to the king and tell him about me."

They said to the king: "One Mother Alaguz does not know where to spend the night. She said: 'If he lets me stay here, I will stay, and if he does not, I will lie down till I die.'"

The king said to them: "Go and bring her in. Old women say sweet things. Tell the king's sick daughter, and maybe, with God's help, the king's daughter will answer."

She entered, as has been told. She kissed the hand and the head of his wife, who was sitting next to him.

She said to them: "What happened to you? Why are you sitting there, stunned and sad, why do you not laugh and play?"

He said to her: "Oh Mother Alaguz! I was barren and did not beget children until I begot one daughter. And she does not talk and does not allow anyone to enter her room. They bring her food and close the door." She said to him: "I will go to her. I will go and dance for her, and I will go and sing for her, and I will do everything to make her talk."

Good. They took her to her room. When she entered, she was sitting on a chair. When she saw Mother Alaguz, she threw herself on the bed, covered herself, and pretended she was asleep.

—"Oh the king's daughter, good evening, oh the king's daughter."

But the king's daughter does not answer.

They brought her some tea.

—"The king's daughter! Have a cup of tea, maybe you have not had anything to drink today."

No answer.

They brought them supper. Mother Alaguz ate.

—"The king's daughter, rise and have supper, maybe you have not had anything to eat today. The king's daughter, the king's daughter." But there was no answer.

So what did Mother Alaguz do? She looked around and noticed that the king's daughter was staring at a wardrobe.

Mother Alaguz said to herself: "Good, there is something in that wardrobe. I will not go to sleep tonight."

She wrapped herself up in her scarf and left a chink open through which she watches this daughter of a king. A tiny, tiny chink. It was night. Nobody goes upstairs, and nobody goes downstairs. The king's daughter took the key that was on top of the wardrobe, opened the wardrobe, and took out a boy who was so beautiful that he would say to the sun: "You shine, or else I will shine. The God that created you created me."

He fell on her, kisses and embraces her, kisses and embraces, and she, too, kissed and embraced him. He lifted her on his shoulders, and they danced, ate, and drank. They played, they danced, they sang; there was nothing they did not do.

When the crier started calling,[3] he said to her: "That's enough."

She put him into the wardrobe. She locked him up and put the small key on top of the wardrobe and pretended she was asleep.

Then Mother Alaguz said to herself: "Now I too will go to sleep."

In the morning, they brought them some tea.

---

[3] The narrator is referring to the muezzin who calls Muslims to morning prayers.

—"The king's daughter, good morning, maybe you stayed awake at night, and maybe you are hungry . . . "

No answer.

Mother Alaguz drank her tea and went downstairs.

The king said to her: "Mother Alaguz, did she speak to you? Was there anything she talked about? Did she utter a word?"

She said to him: "Sir, the king's daughter talked to the one she loves, and those she does not love she does not talk to."

The king's wife rose. She said to her: "Mother Alaguz, you should be ashamed to say these things! Her door is locked. Nobody can get to her. Nobody goes to her, and nobody comes."

She said to them: "Shut up! I am the one who knows everything. And now, may God leave you in peace."

—"Oh Mother Alaguz, sit down. Here is some money, take it. Here is some tea, take it. Here is some salted butter, take it."

She said to them: "I will not take anything. I will take nothing. The penny I dropped, give it to me."

They gave her her penny. She left. She walked, and she walked, and she walked. It grew dark again. Rain came. Wind came, a storm came, and it was night. She keeps on walking, and nothing matters to her except walking. Again she arrives at the door of the king's house. The guards rose and said to her: "Oh Mother Alaguz! Is this the time for a human being to arrive? The sky is black, and there are storms."

She said to them: "My feet carried me here, and I just bow my head and walk. And now speak to the king and tell him about me. If he says 'Let her come!' you send for me, and if he does not say 'Let her come,' I will sleep here, and if I die, may God be with me and grant me peace."

They spoke to the king and told him about her. The king said to them: "Go and send her in!"

When they sent her in they said to her: "Mother Alaguz, be careful, perhaps the king will see you and kill you."

She said to them: "Why?"

They said to her: "The king and all the town are in mourning, do you not see that the whole town is black and in mourning, and the king is in mourning, and his wives are in mourning, his servant girls are in mourning, and you are wearing your white, clean scarf, be careful, lest they put you in jail."

She said to them: "Just let me in, and the rest is none of your business."

Good, she came before the king, she kissed his hand, she kissed his head.

—"May God grant you safety, why do you mourn? The king never mourns. Why? Tell me why, and perhaps with God's help salvation will come through me and we'll see what is to be done."

The king said to her: "What can I tell you? Let it be, Mother Alaguz, and keep silent."

She said to him: "Just tell me. I will not leave before you tell me what happened to you. Why does the whole town mourn, and why do you mourn?"

He said to her: "Oh Mother Alaguz, I married a hundred women but one, and for twelve years I did not beget a child. And this woman is the hundredth. There is nothing I did not do: I visited the tombs of the saints, and I took medicine, and this woman bore me a child. When he was fourteen years old, he went hunting with the guards. He hunted the first day, he hunted the second day, and on the third day he did not return with them. And now four years have gone by since he left, and he must be eighteen. I lost three or four thousand men when I had the mountains, hills, and valleys searched. I was hoping they might find him, find the bones of the horse. Nothing. The search parties do not return, wolves prey on them. And now that I have not found him for four years, the whole town mourns him."

She said to him: "My lord, I will say two words."

He said to her: "What, oh Mother Alaguz?"

She said to him: "Rise, send a town crier. All the houses are to be painted, one house green and the next white, and the whole town will be whitewashed. And you have your house whitewashed, and take off you mourning clothes, you and your wife and the servant girls, wash and put on clean clothes and clean the streets. And all will be well."

—"Oh Mother Alaguz, what is the meaning of what you are saying?"

She said to him: "I will tell you the most important thing later. You just do as I told you, and you will see."

He went and sent the town crier, as I said before. He decreed: "Listen! Everybody must paint his house either green or white."

The world was bright and shining. All the houses were whitewashed. They woke, they drank tea. The king drank tea, and they gave Mother Alaguz tea.

She said to him: "Of all your helpers, who do you love best? Do you love the Kadi best, or the vizier, or the deputy vizier? Take what is most dear to you and be on your way."

The king rode on one side, the vizier on the other, and Mother

Alaguz was in the middle. Forward, forward, forward. And they asked about the town about which, when leaving it, Mother Alaguz asked: "What is the name of the town where the king's daughter won't talk?"

They said to her: "The name is Ḥalama, the city of Ḥalama."[4]

They looked for the city of Ḥalama, on and on and on, until they found it. When they wanted to enter the town, she said to him, to the king: "I will tell you two words."

He said to her: "Which words, oh Mother Alaguz?"

She said to him: "Are you and the king of Ḥalama close friends?"

He said: "Yes."

—"In what way are you close?"

"We used to ride on horseback, to wander about to see kings, to throw parties and to talk to them."

She said to him: "Good, go and ask them: 'Where is the king of Ḥalama?' till they show him to you. When you go to see him, kiss him. When he says to you: 'Why did you come, oh king? Welcome! For what reason did you come?' tell him: 'I want to have a look at your house and build one like it. I wanted to send emissaries, but I feared they would not understand the plan of the house, and therefore I have come by myself.' And when he takes you and wants to open the last room for you, say to him: 'No, open the room in the middle for me.' When he opens it, start walking around and observing from a small opening above. Take him aside and say: 'This door, where does it lead?' Do not mention the word "wardrobe." Just open the wardrobe, and bring the youth that is in there."

He said to her: "Oh Mother Alaguz, and if I do not find the key?"

She said to him: "The key is there, just lift your eyes."

He went, as has been narrated, and came to the king, the king of Ḥalama. "My lord, what is it you wish? Why did you yourself come here?"

He said to him: "My friend, I was told about your house and about the decorations, and I wanted to build a house like that, and I was afraid to send a messenger, and that is why I myself came."

He said to him: "Welcome, welcome, welcome, come in. Drink tea."

He said to him: "I won't drink before I have seen the house."

He went, as has been narrated, showed him the house. He

---

[4] A legendary place.

wanted to open the last room. He said to him: "No! Open the room in the middle. People only want to see the middle part, but they do not take any notice of [the rooms] at the end."

He opened the room in the middle for him. He and the vizier entered the room. They walked about, he lifted his eyes and lo and behold! he sees the small key. He picked it up. He said: "This door—where does it lead?" He opened the door, and the youth jumped on him. He lifted him on his shoulders and danced with him, danced, danced. But the king of Ḥalama fell down; he fainted.

He said to him: "King of Ḥalama!"

He said to him: "Yes."

He said to him: "Your daughter is a whore. You say: 'She is sick, she won't talk and does not let anyone in!' I have been sending out search parties for four years, and they do not return. Wolves ate them; demons tore them to pieces. The whole world looks for my son, on the hills and in the valleys, and she—hid him in the wardrobe?! If she had been my daughter, I would have cut her up into four pieces, and would have her thrown into the sea."

The unhappy king was shame-faced; the poor man had no answer.

He said to him: "Oh almighty God, may God not burn the liver.[5] This is the only daughter we have."

He said to him: "I married a hundred women but one, until finally [the hundredth wife] bore me this son. I had to look for him; it took me four years to find him. I will proclaim that people may no longer be tried by you, and your government will no longer be allowed to rule. Get rid of this daughter; she is corrupt."

Good. He took his son and left.

—"My lord, I will give you my daughter, even if she is going to be a servant. She got used to your son . . ."

He said to him: "Be quiet so I don't cut off your head with this sword."

He took the youth and put him on the horse's back, he took Mother Alaguz and danced with her all the way, until she said: "That's enough."

When they came to town he sent the proclamation to let the

---

[5] According to folk belief, love and hatred are located in the liver. When a loved one is harmed, the liver undergoes a change, as though it is burned. In Arabic, there is a metaphor to express the wish that no harm should come to the beloved, i.e., that his liver should not be burned. In Hebrew there too are expressions that reflect the folk belief that feelings are located in inner parts of the body such as kidneys and heart. God is characterized as "Boḥen Klayot Va'lev"—He who sees what is in the kidneys and hearts of people.

A hanger of a memorial candle, Ner Neshama, the beginning of the twentieth century. By kind permission of the Israel Museum, Jerusalem.

people know that the king's son had been found. Everybody came running to see the king's son. The horses run about, people play games, the orchestra plays, the songs, the flags and the women yell.

Good, at last the people dispersed, they left.

The king said: "Oh my son."

He said to him: "Yes."

He said to him: "Don't you leave the house. You will learn how to rule. The day will come, and I will die, and the money and the property will be left, and there won't be anyone to inherit it. You must learn to rule in my stead.

Good, that is how it was. The son followed him everywhere. On, and on, and on. One month passed, two months. One night as they were sitting [in the room], the king of Ḥalama came. He brought two oxen, put his daughter and his wife on a mule, and brought two camels laden with salted butter, honey, oil, all kinds of good things, and thus he came.

The guard asked: "What is it you want?"

He said to him: "Call the king."

The guard went to the king, and said to him: "My lord, my lord, put your hand on your head and say: 'I forgive.'"

He said to him: "God will forgive you if you tell the truth."

He said to him: "There is a man with a woman and a girl on a mule, and he rides a mule and there are two oxen with him."

The king said to his wife: "That is the king of Ḥalama. He has

51

brought his daughter in order to entreat me to marry my son to her." He left [the room], as has been narrated, and found the king of Ḥalama.

The king of Ḥalama fell upon him and kissed his head.

—"Oh my lord! Hide what God has hidden. Oh my lord! Hide what The Creator has hidden. We are both kings. This is the only daughter I have. And we did not want to impose our will on her. And she is used to your son and loves him. And now let her be a servant in your kitchen, provided only that he weds her, so people say: 'She married a king.' If you want her, she will stay with you, and if you don't want her, I will come and take her away. Provided that she is considered as a person that is married to a king."

Good, as has been narrated they had a big wedding, and there is no one greater than God. She stayed there and lived with him. He built her a house. And the king's son also married the minister's daughter and built a house for her. Good, so they live and eat and drink. And the tale flows with the rivers. And our friends are generous givers.

## *Commentary:* IFA 16434

### THE TALES OF MOTHER ALAGUZ

This folktale is a conglomerate of several narrative types held together by the frame-story of Mother Alaguz and her wanderings. The stories are set where Mother Alaguz breaks her journeys, and she solves the problems arising in each tale. The first tale (The Demon Woman) constitutes an independent inner story with a self-contained plot. But the second story (The Silent Princess) and the third story (The Lost Prince) are interrelated and complement each other.

The structure is therefore as follows:

| THE TALE OF THE WANDERINGS OF MOTHER ALAGUZ | | |
|---|---|---|
| Station I | Station II | Station III |
| The Tale of the Demon Woman | The Tale of the Silent Princess | The Tale of the Lost Prince |

The tale is unique, and in this composition—an old woman who leads a vagrant life solves the problems of those whom she encounters in her travels—there is no parallel in IFA. Generally, tales structured in this manner belong to Aarne-Thompson 874, "The Proud King is Won." In the tales that belong to this narrative type a girl falls in love with a proud prince who refuses to marry her unless she performs certain seemingly impossible tasks. The protagonist meets the challenge, goes on a journey, and wherever she stops she copes with the problems facing her, and finally she wins the hand of the prince in marriage. The versions listed by Aarne-Thompson were recorded in the Mediterranean cultural area: Italy (Sicily), Yugoslavia, Turkey. Eberhard and Boratav list eighteen versions.[1] IFA has six versions of the narrative type, from Greece, Morocco, Libya, Syria, Israel Sefardi, and Turkey.[2]

The frame-story opens with the birth of Mother Alaguz, indicating that she has been singled out for something special in her life. Her birth was not an ordinary one. She was born clutching an object (a penny) that had some bearing on her future life (Motif N 121.1). The object was to support her as long as she lived. As a result, she is independent and self-assured; indeed, these qualities stand out as she wanders from one place to another while negotiating with personages greater and more powerful than she.

The penny also adds a humoristic dimension to the tale as a whole. The frame-story tells us how this coin supports her, as vendors refuse to sell her anything for a penny and prefer to give her merchandise for free so she can keep her penny; the inner story establishes the disproportion between the gifts offered to Mother Alaguz by the kings she had helped on the one hand, and her determination to hold on to her penny on the other hand. This disproportion makes for a comic effect.

Clearly this disproportion further highlights the independence and self-assurance of Mother Alaguz: he who is content with a penny and needs no regal present is truly independent.

It may be asked why the story-teller chose to place the inner stories in which tasks must be accomplished within a frame-story whose protagonist is an old woman, whilst in narrative type Aarne-Thompson 874 tasks are assigned to a young girl who wants a proud bridegroom to marry her.

---

[1] Eberhard, and Boratav, 1953, 188.

[2] From Greece IFA 10094, published in Attias 1976, no. 7; from Libya IFA 5528, published in Noy 1967, no. 63; from Turkey IFA 12503, published in Alexander and Noy 1989, no. 63.

The answer links up with the personality of the story-teller, Ḥaviva Dayan. In spite of her great age (she was eighty years old when she narrated the story), Ḥaviva Dayan was a very active woman who helped with the housework and also did some sewing. She was a woman with a strong personality, and in her opinion she was equipped to assist and counsel all the members of her family in times of trouble and distress.

At the same time, Ḥaviva Dayan was fully aware of the change in status of the elderly due to the transition from the traditional Moroccan way of life to life in the modern State of Israel, and she mentioned this repeatedly when she spoke to us. The transition to Israeli culture made the elderly feel helpless. Most of them did not acquire the Hebrew language, and they remained strangers to the rules of conduct of the new culture and unable to deal with Israeli institutions. As many of them had no income of their own, they were totally dependent on the younger members of the family.

Our story, in which the old woman is the protagonist who does not depend on anyone because she is lucky, frugal, wise, sly, and resourceful, depicts the kind of heroism that reflects the story-teller's wishes.

It is no accident that Type Aarne-Thompson 874 was chosen to this end. In stories belonging to this type generally an old woman assists and advises the young, inexperienced girl-protagonist (Motif H 1233.1.1). The recollection of these stories, in which an old woman has a counselling role, caused the story-teller to introduce an old protagonist, an old woman who is not afraid of neither natural disasters nor powerful rulers or supernatural beings and who accomplishes all her tasks thanks to these qualities. In fact the mighty and powerful need her help and advice, without which they would be lost. This reflects the secret wish of the narrator: to go back in time and regain the position of honor the old occupied in traditional society, to be the helper and decision maker to whom everybody turns for advice and assistance.

When Ḥaviva Dayan narrates Mother Alaguz's stories, she narrates herself: she relates a fascinating, frightening, and enjoyable story with which she interweaves her own wishes, the wishes of an old Jewish woman who has lived through changes of fortune and changes of culture, and who wants an honored place in present-day Israeli society, both for herself and for other people like her.

# *Never Trust the Dark Haired Man*

### From: Ḥaviva Dayan

It has been related [that] God is everywhere. And there was a Ḥakham.[1] Now about this Ḥakham, poor fellow: he did not beget any children. He taught children, and he felt very much alone. He and his wife are all by themselves.

Let's get on with the story, let's get on. One day the wife is sitting (in her room), and a Jewish woman comes and says: "Good morning, Ḥakham's wife."

She said to her: "Good morning."

She said to her: "Where is the Ḥakham?"

She said to her: "In the synagogue. He is teaching the children. What do you want him for?"

She said to her: "I have been told that he writes about begetting children,[2] and I want him to write something about it for me too because I don't have any children."

She said: "I see. He writes amulets for other people so they should have children, but he does not write any amulets for himself so he should have children!"

The woman kept silent and pretended she was dying. He woke her: "Oh my daughter, what is wrong with you? Oh my daughter, with whom have you been quarreling? Is there anything you want? I will buy it. Is there anything you want? I will get it for you."

She said to him: "I did not quarrel with anyone, I didn't. And you live here with me, and you deceive me and you double-cross me."

He said to her: "Why?"

She said to him: "You write [amulets] for everybody so they should have children, and we—you do not write [any amulets] for us so we should have children? And my dear friend[3] knows what begetting children involves."

He said to her: "My daughter, prepare a dream question, and

---

[1] This is a term for a rabbi, used by Moroccan Jews in ancient Hebrew.

[2] The narrator is referring to fertility amulets.

[3] She means the rabbi.

put on a new dress, and go to the ritual bath and do your hair and put on make-up and use some perfume and I, I will do the same, and let's see what the Maggid[4] is going to tell us."

She did so. The next day she washed the floors, prepared an early supper, washed, went to the ritual bath, and put on a new dress. He came too. He shaved his head. He washed. He went to the ritual bath, and he returned home. They had supper and went to sleep. The Maggid appeared to them.

He said: "What is it you want, oh Ḥakham? If you want a daughter, she will convert on her wedding day; she will become a Muslim. If you want a son, he will be luckless; he will not have any luck."

He rose, he said to her: "You who knowest no evil, here is what I dreamt."

She said to him: "I dreamt the same thing."

He said to her: "What do you want?"

She said to him: "I want the girl. I insist."

He said to her: "Oh God! Oh my daughter! Here I am, a renowned Ḥakham: am I to beget a daughter that converts to Islam on her wedding day? And the rabbis stand and watch, and the whole world stands and watches as she converts to Islam? What am I going to feel in my heart? We want a boy. We will support him. If he is unlucky and cannot make a living, we will keep him and his wife and his children, and our reward will be the observance of the commandment of circumcision, of redemption of the firstborn, of finding him a wife. And when we die we will leave him everything. But a girl will convert, and she will live with the Muslims. What good is that going to be to us? None whatsoever. We will have to leave all our property to the gentiles."

She said to him: "But I want a girl. I insist."

He said to her: "If he asks you first, you tell him 'a girl,' and if he asks me first I will tell him 'a boy.'"

They slept. He appeared to them.

He said to him: "Scholar, what is it you want? Do you want a boy, or do you want a girl?"

He said to him: "I want a boy, and if my wife says she wants a girl, tell her 'no.'"

He came to her, and he said to her: "My daughter, what do you want?"

She said to him: "I want a girl. I insist."

---

[4] A bearer of news, God's messenger in ancient Hebrew who has a central function in Jewish mysticism.

He said to her: "The Ḥakham wants a boy. You have no right to ask for a girl."

And so he left. The woman became pregnant. Three months—getting fat, three months—on heat, three months—she grabs the rope, and she cries: "Oh He who saves from trouble! May he save her from her troubles!" Then she bore a boy of radiant beauty.

They had him circumcised, they performed the ceremony of the redemption of the firstborn, and the child started studying the Tora. He grew up. His father was his teacher, and time went by, went by, went by.

One day the students who studied with his father appeared. They came to see the youth. The Ḥakham was not at home. The youth said: "Come in!"

They said to him: "Your father is wealthy, he has a lot of money, and he does not have any other children to support. You are the only son. Tell him to give you money, and go with us. We will buy merchandise for you, and we will put the merchandise in stores, and then we will go out again. We are tired of studying."

His father came home. He saw the boy; the boy was crying.

He said to him: "What happened, my boy? With whom did you quarrel? Who said anything to you? Do you want money? Is there anything you want?"

He said to him: "I do not want anything. I want to go with the two youths who were your students. I want to go with them. I want to leave, and you—give me money for my travel expenses."

The proverb says: "When he picked him up he thought he was as soft as a soft stone, but when he put him down he was as hard as flint." And again: "He found that his head was harder than a stone."[5]

He said to him: "Go out and call those youths."

He called them.

He said to them: "You take good care of him, and I will give him money, and if you do not bring him back alive, you will get ten years in prison. Ten years."

They said to him: "We will personally bring him back to you, and we will buy goods and bring him back. . . ."

He said to him: "How much money?"

He said to him: "Six thousand," and he gave him six thousand.

He left together with them. On and on, they boarded a ship. They came to a city and bought goods there. When they stepped off the ship, the youth looked up, and there—he notices a large syna-

---

[5] These are two Arabic proverbs. Both imply that the father thought he would be able to talk the boy out of going away, but the boy was firm.

gogue, and on its walls there is Hebrew lettering. Inside the synagogue there are Muslims and Christians, and Jews too. Many people had gathered there. The youth says: "This is a Jewish synagogue, why are these Muslims here, and these soldiers, and these Jewish rabbis, and these guards, and all the rest?" But no matter whom he approaches, nobody wants to answer.

Then the youth said to someone: "Here is some money so you can buy cigarettes. Now tell me why there are Muslims in this synagogue which is meant for Jewish rabbis only?"

He said to him: "There was a certain Ḥakham who owed a certain Muslim four thousand, and when the Ḥakham died they buried him in the yard of the synagogue so the Muslim should not find him. But someone told the Muslim, who has now arrived here, saying he will disinter the Jew and bury him in the cave (that is, the Muslim cemetery). Only then will he cancel the debt of four thousand."

He said to him: "Call this Muslim."

He called him.

He said to him: "What do you want from the Ḥazzan[6] who is buried here?"

He said to him: "He owed me four thousand, and now I have written off the debt. But I will remove his body and bury him in our cemetery."

He said to him: "Even if I have to kill you and cut up your body together with the bodies of all the other Muslims, I will not let you touch the body of this Ḥazzan. If I were a local resident, I would grab you by the neck and throw you to the ground. And now, scram, and here is your four thousand."

He gave him the four thousand, and the Muslim departed.

The Ḥakham's son said: "Are there any members of the burial society around?"

He said: "There are some."

They took the body of the Jew and carried it to the Jewish cemetery. The Ḥakham's son looked around, walking first in one direction and then in another until finally he found a section where rabbis were buried.

He said to them: "This is where I want you to bury the Ḥakham."

They dug a grave next to where Jewish rabbis were buried. They carried the body there. They buried him. He had a tomb constructed. He paid laborers. He went to the synagogue. They cleaned

---

[6] Arabs call rabbis 'Ḥazzan,' literally-Cantor.

the synagogue, tidied it up. He lit candles. They finished all the work. He stayed behind.

He said: "Woe! My friends probably bought the goods and left, and my father probably blames them; he may even have imprisoned them! What am I to do? I do not know where to go and how to return (home)."

The Ḥakham's son was standing next to the synagogue. Now there was nobody there anymore; they had all gone home. But a child was passing by, and he called : "Boy, come here!"

He said to him: "Leave me alone, I cannot stay because the ship may set sail and I will be left behind."

He said to him: "I, too, am going on board ship; I implore you, take me with you. I do not know my way."

He took him with him. He came to the ship. He rented space on the ship and was getting ready to go on board when someone comes and cries: "Who would like to buy a ship?"

He said to him: "How much?"

He said to him: "A thousand pounds."

He said to him: "What kind of cargo?"

He said: "Straw. Gold. I will not tell you what cargo. If you find the cargo is straw, may God help you, and if you find it is gold, may God help you."

He bought it. As I have told you, he gave him the little money he had left. He took over the ship. And he sailed, sailed, sailed. Finally, he came to his home town, and he said: "Call my father."

People said to his father: "Your son has arrived and has brought a ship."

They told his father. But the father had fallen out with the other youths who had returned, and they had been imprisoned for three or four months. And he wore mourning and so did his wife, and they were staying (at home).

They said: "Maybe he is dead, or he was swept away by a stream, or someone killed him. He will never come back." They wore mourning. He no longer prayed, he no longer studied, and he did not do anything.

They said to him: "Ḥakham! Your son has arrived."

He said to them: "Leave me alone. You are telling me a lie. My son is probably dead, or rotting in his grave, or . . ."

They said to him: "Rise. Look at him."

They hurried, wearing their mourners' clothes, till they were face to face with him. The father lifted him onto his shoulders and turned round and was happy, and the women yelled. All the town was there.

And they took him home, they invited the Jewish women, they invited the Jewish men. They brought liquor flavored with aniseed, dried fruit, everything. Good, they ate, they drank, and they went home.

The son said: "Oh my father, open the hold of the ship. Let's see what is inside."

He opened the hold of the ship. As he was hitting the ship with a hammer, a woman called out.

She said to him: "Spare me. I am a human being."

So they started working until they were able to pull out a beautiful girl who says to the sun: "Shine, or I will shine on God who created me." This girl sat down with them. When he wanted to go to the synagogue, she said to him: "I will go with you."

So she would go with him and with his father and pray in the synagogue and then return home. They would have dinner together and eat together, and so on, and so on. For two or three months. Then the Ḥakham's wife rose. She said to him: "Ḥakham!"

He said: "Yes."

She said to him: "Now this girl—he brought her, and he bought her, let us ask him if he wants to marry her. We need not find him a strange girl. If she stays in this house, it would be an insult."

The Ḥakham said to her: "Oh my daughter! I will not speak to her, you go and tell her, and if she agrees, tell me."

It was dinner time, and the woman said: "My daughter, come here. Do you want to marry my son? If you do, we will do everything for you, we will build you a house next to ours, and I will cook, and you will come and have meals and leave."

The girl said to her: "Whatever you decide, I will accept it."

She called her son and said the same thing to him too.

The son said to her: "Mother, whatever you do, whatever you decide, I will accept it."

Then they prepared, they arranged a big wedding, and there is no one greater than God; he and his wife sat there. They built a house next to their own. He would come in the evening and eat supper and go back home, and he would come for his midday meal and go back home.

On and on, on and on. She started having children. She had her first child. She had her second child. She had a daughter. Good, she was sitting there, when her first child started standing up, and she said to her husband: "Come on, I know how to use the tools used in weaving, and now you go and tell your father you want him to lend you a hundred pounds. I will buy silk, I will hand sew the cloth and sell (my work), and what I earn I will give to these children. It is a disgrace to ask your father (for money); let me (earn money) so I can give them something, let me contribute, just let me."

The husband said to her: "All right." He went to see his father. His father lent him a hundred pounds. He took her to the silk merchants, and he bought some silk. The silk merchant said to him: "When she finishes weaving, bring me the finished goods so I can buy them from you."

Good, he brought her the silk thread. She would do the weaving, using two or three weaving tools, and she would give him the cloth, and he would go and sell it. She repaid the one hundred pounds, and there was some money left so she could buy silk thread and work. And when some money was left, she would spend it on food and clothing for her family and for herself. Good, she led a quiet life, she eats, she drinks. Then she started having children again. She had another daughter. When he wanted to buy her some more silk, she said to him: "Take care, you son of a Hakham! Don't you ever bring the dark haired man to this house." She knows that she is the daughter of the king of the Christians, that she was stolen, put on the ship and sold. She was afraid her father might come and look for her . . .

She said to him: "Don't you ever allow the one with the dark head of hair into this house. Don't let him sleep here, and don't let him eat here, ever."

So he departed, and he forgot what she had told him. He took her work to the same Jewish merchant, and bought her silk, and when there was some money left he bought things for the children. She bought clothes; she bought clothes for him and for herself. She left nothing undone. She had a daughter, she had two sons. Good, she was at home and lived a peaceful life.

And her father came and looked for her. From one town to another did the king of the Christians travel. He was looking for his daughter. Whenever he was in a new town he would say: "Show me the silk dealers." And they would show him the silk dealers. Then he would say to them: "Does nobody bring weaving tools here in order to sell them?" They would tell him: "We do not know what 'weaving tools' are. What is that, 'weaving tools'?" He would say to them: "They are called 'weaving tools.' Does nobody come here in order to sell them to you?" They would say: "No."

On and on, on and on, on and on, until he came to that town. He begged someone, saying to him: "Please take us to the silk dealers." He took him to the silk dealers. When he came to the first dealer, he found these very things hanging [from the ceiling]. He said: "This is the town where my daughter is living."

He walked up to the storekeeper and said to him: "Good morning." He said to him: "Good morning." He said to him: "Satisfied with the person who sat next to you, oh my son!" He said to him: "Does the country belong to me? The country belongs to the government! Sit here till you get tired." He said to him: "Who do you buy this woven material from?" He said to him: "A certain man sells it to me. He will be coming here right now. He always comes at this time." He said to him: "How much do you pay for them?" He said to him: "I pay two hundred pounds a piece." He said to him: "He really sells cheap. Where I come from, we pay a thousand pounds a piece, and they are hard to come by." "Good," he said. "When is he going to be here?" He said to him: "You will see him right away."

He stepped behind the store. He took off his white suit and put on a dirty, threadbare suit with holes in it, full of whitewash, with patches all over. He also put on torn shoes, and took off his own shoes, put on a hat and sat down.

And right then the man came. He brought the silken cloth and sold it. When he left, he followed him. They came to the house of the son of the Ḥakham. When the Ḥakham's son was about to close the door, he said to him: "Whatever you do will be regarded as an act of charity. I am starving. Be charitable and let me spend the night here, behind this door."

He was moved. He told him to come in. They sat next to the door. He boiled some water for him. He made him a small pot of tea. He took a small cup and poured him some tea. The king in disguise said to him: "May the hardships, life has in store for you, be my hardships." He poured him a small cup of tea and offered it to him. He said [to the Ḥakham's son]: "May the hardships, life has in store for you, be my hardships instead. The good things in life stay with the person that enjoys them. Why don't you join me? Get yourself a small cup, we'll pour you some tea, and you sit next to me."

He fetched a small cup of tea. And then he put a sleeping draught in the cup. He put the sleeping draught in the same cup. He placed the first cup in his hand, and poured tea in the cup he had fetched, and drank it. When the Ḥakham's son drank the tea, he fell over like a log.

Then the king of the Christians took his suitcase and stepped into the room and said to her: "My daughter!"

She said to him: "Father, you have come all the way here . . ."

Her father said to her: "I would have traveled even farther for your sake. Take your children, and take all that is dear to you, and take your things, and let's go."

She said to him: "And my husband?"

Her father answered: "Your husband dropped dead, may God rest his soul."

She collected her things and her children's things. She put them in suitcases and took her children. He carried the suitcases and one child, and she took the girl and the boy by the hand, and they left.

On and on, on and on, they arrived in their town. Good, they stayed there.

Let us return to the Ḥakham's son. The Ḥakham came home and said to his wife: "Tell me, our son did not come to the synagogue today, where is he?"

The wife said to him: "The children did not come for tea either. They usually come early! They did not come and have tea."

They went over to their son's house and knocked on the door, but there was no answer. They knocked, and they knocked, and they knocked. They called a carpenter. They opened the door. They found him. They lifted him up, and they called a doctor. He woke, he had something to eat and something to drink, and he said to them: "Where is my wife? And where are my children?"

The parents said to him: "Oh our son, this is what we are asking you! This is what happened. You did not come to the synagogue today, and the children did not show up, so we came here to find out what befell you."

He said to them: "The town to which she has been taken does not let me stay here. I will go where she went."

His father thought he was a soft stone, but he found that his head was harder than stone.

The father said to him: "You have just come to. Wait a day, and leave tomorrow. We won't stop you."

Good, he waited a day. He rested. The next day, his mother gave him food for the journey. She gave him some bread, or some chicken, or whatever. He walked, and he walked. He would walk in the wilderness, in the desert, on the hills and in all those other places . . . in the forests there are snakes, scorpions—everything . . . and he keeps walking, walking, walking, and he feels his way blindly . . . in the mountains, in the hills. And he sees a man. The man is standing there.

The man says to him: "Come, my son, where are you going? Nobody has ever come this way before! Why are you here? Where are you going, what happened to you?"

He said to him: "Leave me alone."

The man said to him: "Tell me, just tell me. Maybe I can help you."

He said to him: "Let me be. Just let me be."

He pleaded with him, pleaded with him, pleaded with him, and finally he said to him: "Good. Go, there is a road leading to another road in that direction. And there will be rain, and thunderbolts, and clouds, and fog."

He said: "Woe unto me! Why did I not listen to that Jewish man! I will return to him."

He returned to him.

The man said to him: "Good. Now that you have come back, tell me what is bothering you."

He said to him: "A man drugged me, and took away my wife and children, and I do not know who did it."

The man said to him: "Good. If you promise you will give me the wife, you can have the children, and I will send you to her town; a distance of seventy years separates you from it.

He said to him: "No."

The man said to him: "Then you give me the children, and you can keep the woman."

He said: "No."

He kept pleading with him.

Finally the rabbi's son said to him: "I will let you have the children."

The man said to him: "Then I will give you something, my son. Here is a small carpet. You sit on it, and it will carry you to where they are. Close your eyes, and open them, and you will find yourself in that city. When you see a large dung heap, hit it with this stick and say:

Go away, dung heap.
Come here, orchard,
Bear fruit in season
Bear fruit out of season.

And here is a hat: wear it, and you will see other people, but they will not see you. But I want you to return all these things. I am going to stay here and wait for you to bring your wife and children, and then you will return them to me."

He said to him: "All right."

He stepped on the little carpet, sat down on it, and found himself in that city. He entered, hit [the dung heap] with the stick, and a garden sprang up (God, let me see the garden). There were fishes, ponds, fruit, flowers, mint, everything.

They put up proclamations telling the townspeople and the whole world: "A garden has sprung up all on its own. Come and visit the garden . . ."

Her father, the king of the Christians, was the first to arrive. The son of the Jewish Ḥakham recognized him and said to himself: "This is the one who spent a night in our home." The son of the Ḥakham put on the hat and could see people without being seen by them.

Her father went and told his family at home.

—"Oh my father! you went there and saw it all, but I—ever since you brought me here I and the children have not been out of the house, and I have not seen anything," the girl said to him. "Now let me go and see . . ."

Her father said to her: "Oh my daughter! What if your husband is there?"

She said to him: "Where is my husband? He is probably dead, and even if he is not dead, he has no money for the journey, and even if he did have the money, he would not know how to get here . . . He knows how to get to the synagogue, and he knows the way back home. That is all he knows. Even if he can raise the money, he possesses no cunning so he cannot come to this city."

Good, she went there, and she visited the garden. When she entered, he threw the hat on both her head and his head, and took her hands.

The wife said to him: "So you did get here?"

The husband said to her: "I got as far as this city, and I would even go farther for your sake. Where are the children? How are you? And how did all this happen?"

She said to him: "Didn't I tell you that you must not allow the dark haired man to set foot in our house? You brought all this upon yourself! When he said to you 'I would like to sit down here', you ought to have said 'No', and you ought to have told him he should go outside with the teapot and drink his tea there, and go away!"

The husband said to her: "And what next?"

She said to him: "What am I going to do now?"

He said to her: "Now you go to your father. Sit down and weep and say to him: 'These children have never been out, they have never had a good time and they have never seen the town. Now I want seven days off. I will get a tent, the servant girl can come along, she will put up the tent and she will take me food, she will carry the food there, and she will carry it back again, till the seven days are over, and I will take the children and be there by myself.'"

Good, she went home and started crying. Her father came. He said to her: "What happened?"

She said to him: "Father, ever since we came here I and the children have never been out. They have never seen the world, they have never seen this city. And now, I want seven days off."

Her father said to her: "Oh my daughter, I fear for your safety, lest your husband should be out there . . ."

She said to him: "I told you my husband is probably dead. He does not have the money to come here, and even if does, he would not know how to get to this city. He goes to the synagogue and back home. That is all he knows. Give me a servant girl, give me a tent, I will put it up and the girl will bring me my midday meal and my supper and go home again, and when the seven days are over she will come and fold the tent, and I will take the children and come back home."

Her father said to her: "All right."

She left and got the tent and put it up. The servant girl carried her tea, and carried her supper, she carried her food. Her husband put on the hat; they were all covered by the hat, and nobody could see them. They could see people, but people could not see them.

On and on, on and on, on and on till the seven days were over. Seven days went by. He rose and made an announcement: "All the people must leave because the owner wants to bring electricity to the garden. Those who stay will have to pay a fine."

Good, everybody was afraid. They left. On and on, on and on. The next day the garden was empty. The next morning the servant came and brought them some tea.

She said to her: "Good, take the cups, the cushions, the carpet, the blankets—remove everything from the tent. Then you will fold the tent, and I will take the children, and we shall leave."

Good, they carried everything back to the house. He carried the carpet, and he spread it for them. The children sat down. He carried the suitcases. For when he had said to her: "Tell your father you want seven days off," he had said: "Take everything, take the children's things, and if you want something from your father's house and some gold or whatever, put it in suitcases. You can't go back."

Good, the suitcases were in the center of the carpet. The children sat down, and she sat down. Then they left. They folded the tent. They put it next to the suitcase. He beat it with a stick and said: "Suitcase, go back, and you, garden, disappear." The suitcase returned. She left the tent there. They closed their eyes and opened them and were standing next to the self-same man who had given him the magic objects.

The servant girl came. She found that they were no longer there. So she left and informed the king.

The king said: "If she left, may God be her guide."

They came to this self-same man. The man said to him: "My son, bless God who has saved you. You have come, you have brought your wife, you have brought your children!"

The Ḥakham's son said to him: "Why? How do you know?"

He said to him: "My son, you must clear your head. Wait till you have recovered, and then tell me who I am."

Good. They sat down and they rested.

The man said to him: "I am the one who gave you the small carpet, and I am the one who gave you the stick with which you conjured up the garden. You said you would give me the children, and keep your wife, and I said to you, 'Take your wife, and give me your children.'"

The Ḥakham's son answered: "No."

He said to him: "Now what is it you want? If you do not want to give me the children, I will take away the little carpet, and it is raining now, the rains are so heavy that neither porters nor camels can carry them, and you will have to stay here until you die."

Good. The man thought and thought and thought.

He said to him: "Here are the children, here they are." He kissed them and handed them over.

The man said to them: "I have to bring them to your doorstep. Close your eyes and open them, and you will be at your doorstep." They took a few steps; they moved away.

He said to him: "Come, my boy, come, come."

He saw that he was crying, and he said to him: "Come, come, here are your children, and here is your wife. You deserve them because you observed a commandment; you saved me when the Muslims wanted to bury me in their cemetery, and you paid the four thousand I owed. I am the Ḥakham who was interred in the yard of the synagogue, and you are the man who observed the commandment and saved me and paid the four thousand and another one thousand for a tombstone. Here are your children, and here is your wife, for a distance of seventy years separated you from her. But for me you would never have seen your children and your wife again. And now—here is your wife, and here are your children."

He kissed them, he blessed them, and they kissed his hands and he blessed the children, and he blessed him.

He said to him: "Good. The favor I am going to do you is this: I will let you ride [on the carpet] to your doorstep because your house is far away. And when you get there, put down the carpet, and put down the stick, and put down the hat you are wearing, for I will follow you, and I will collect them. Don't try to find out who collects them, for when you put them on the ground I will make them disappear; I will take them."

They did so. He came to the doorstep. He put the stick on the ground. He put the carpet on the ground. He tried to turn round, did not find them, they were gone. He knocked on the door. His father came to the door, he was happy, and uttered cries of joy. They took the children, and they danced. They took the woman, and they danced.

Good, there was not a thing they did not do. All the townspeople came; they ate, and they drank, and they did everything. Good, they left.

She said to him: "Good, now don't you ever trust that dark haired man!"

Good, she stayed at home, she wove silk cloth. She sold it. She built a house, raised the children, did everything.

And the tale flowed with rivers,
And my friends are generous givers.

## Commentary: IFA 16431

### NEVER TRUST THE DARK HAIRED MAN

The tale is a conglomerate consisting of two narrative types: the frame-story belongs to narrative type Aarne-Thompson 934*H—"A childless couple may choose between a girl who will suffer and a boy who will be poor all his life." The inner story belongs to the Jewish oicotype Aarne-Thompson 506*C (IFA): "A grateful dead man and the Prophet Elijah as helpers." The frame-story is similar to the folk narrative "What is written in heaven cannot be wiped out," which forms part of the present volume. The narrative type belongs to a group of tales of destiny.

The specially Jewish nature of the folktale as compared with the international folktale lies primarily in the fate awaiting the children to be born. Whereas the international narrative type speaks of suffering and poverty, this folktale speaks of conversion to another faith and bad luck. The genre to which the tale belongs is the sacred legend.

Neora, a tool for rolling strings on spools. By kind permission of the Israel Museum, Jerusalem.

An aura of religious faith is about the characters: the rabbi has the power of writing amulets. The couple observe the rules of purification and ritual immersion. The choice they make—they want a son—will permit them to observe God's commandments, such as circumcision and redemption of the firstborn. Equally, its concept is influenced by faith, the divine sphere and the world of man communicate, and there is divine providence. The infertility of the rabbi's wife is by divine decree; it is God's will that the child be spared a cruel fate in the future, and the divine sphere is revealed through the image of the Maggid who mediates between the two worlds.

The second folktale belongs to the Jewish oicotype Aarne-Thompson 506*C (IFA): "A grateful dead man and the Prophet Elijah as helpers." In IFA there are twelve versions of this narrative type.[1] It seems at first that burial of the dead and the prevention of contempt of the dead are the Jewish underpinnings of this oicotype, but this is not so. Also in the international narrative type Aarne-Thompson 506—"The rescue of the princess"—the hero is re-

---

[1] The versions are from Morocco (5), Sefardi Israel (1), Turkish Kurdistan (1), Iraqi Kurdistan (1), Iraq (2), Persia (1), India (1). Two versions were printed: Avitsuk 1965, no. 23; Shenhar and Bar-Itzhak 1981, no. 4.

deemed when he pays the debts of the deceased whose creditors do not allow him to be buried. Yet it is true that in this folktale, burial is connected with a religious confrontation as the body of the Jew was in danger of being interred in the Muslim cemetery. An investigation of all the folktales in IFA belonging to this oicotype indicates that the feature characterizing the Jewish oicotype is the marriage of the protagonist and a princess who has been rescued from imprisonment and who does beautiful needlework. Although she has warned him, he sells her work, in consequence of which the king, her father, discovers her whereabouts and kidnaps her. The husband who sets out in search of his wife gets help from two supernatural beings: the dead man who had been given a Jewish burial at his direction, and the Prophet Elijah who returns his wife to him.

In our tale a princess is rescued, but the prohibition does not involve the sale of her handiwork but rather a dark haired man who is not to be admitted into their house. The Prophet Elijah, who has a part in most versions of this oicotype, is never mentioned, and the grateful dead man fulfills all the functions of a supernatural helper.

The structure, the absence of the Prophet Elijah, and the magic objects given by the grateful dead man indicate that the tale is in close proximity to the genre of the fairy tale.

An investigation of the tale according to functions and narrative roles suggested by Propp for the Russian fairy tale (Propp 1970) shows that the part of the messenger is present in the story. This part is filled by the youths who persuade the rabbi's son that he should travel with them. In the folk fairy tale, travel symbolizes maturity and the wish to leave one's parents' home, to get married. This is Propp's function, no. 8, and Propp's next function, no. 9, grants the protagonist permission to leave home. Function no. 10—the protagonist leaves home—is his desire to travel.

Another function realized in this tale is no. 12—the protagonist is put to the test. In our tale, the protagonist is placed in a situation where he must decide what to do when a body is being desecrated.

Function no. 13 is the reaction of the protagonist. The protagonist passes the test, and this is expressed by two actions on the plot level: payment of the dead man's debt and Jewish burial.

In consequence of these actions, the protagonist wins the right to marry the princess. But as we are dealing with two combined narrative plots, the order of the functions listed by Propp is changed. The protagonist marries the king's daughter, but he loses her again and must travel again. This part constitutes the explanation of the prophecy of the Maggid prior to the birth of the child, to the effect that the boy would have bad luck.

When he sets out on his travels for the second time, Function no. 14 is realized; this function gives the protagonist the magic objects that, in this tale, are given to him by the grateful dead man.

In function no. 15 the protagonist is transported to where the object of search is located. In the tale, he is transported by means of a magic carpet that had been given to him by the grateful dead man. Fulfilling function no. 16, what had been missing is restored: the wife and the children are returned. And according to function no. 20, the protagonist returns.

The narrative roles are: the messenger (the youths and the father), the protagonist (the rabbi's son), the donor (the grateful dead man), the obstructive character (the king of the Christians), the king's daughter (his wife, the daughter of the king of the Christians).

# MORDEKHAI MALKA

**WHEN WE** recorded the folktales, Mordekhai Malka was about sixty-five years old. He came from the town of Kal'ah in Morocco, where his father Abraham and his mother Simha were living. In the old country, he was a student in a Ḥeder (a place where little children study, literally "a room"), and he earned his living making shoes and peddling.

He came to Israel in 1956 and settled in Shlomi. He was married and had five children.

In the old country, he turned his house into a synagogue. Poor people would come to his house; they would stay there and eat there, and those who knew a story would narrate it. That was how Mordekhai learned his stories. When we recorded him, he did not hear many stories anymore, but he would narrate folktales at home and in the synagogue. According to him, people certainly enjoyed hearing his narratives.

# The King, the Vizier, and the Clever Jew

FROM: MORDEKHAI MALKA

Once upon a time there was a king who held a rabbi in high esteem; he really looked up to him. Whenever the rabbi came to the king, the king would rise from his throne, and ask the rabbi to sit on it.

The king's vizier was jealous and started hating the rabbi. One day he said to himself: "When that rabbi comes, the king rises from his throne and asks him to sit on it, and he neglects me as though I were a dog. How come? What am I going to do about it?"

One day, he said to the king: "Oh sir, oh king, I wish to tell you something."

The king said: "And what is that?"

He said to him: "Why do you rise from your throne and make the rabbi sit on it? We do not like the Jews because they are our enemies, and yet—when the rabbi comes you bow to him and offer him your throne to sit on?!"

He said to him: "Because he is a rabbi and a learned man who knows what is between him and God."

He said to him: "He knows what is between him and God?!"

He said to him: "Yes."

He said to him: "If he knows what is between him and God, I want him to tell me the answers to two questions."

He said to him: "What are they?"

He said to him: "I want him to tell me how many pitchers of water there are in the sea and how many stars in the sky."

—"Aha" said the king. He rose and he sat down. He said to the vizier: "How can he tell you that? You see, this calculation has never been done."

He said to him: "If he is clever and learned and knows what is between him and God, let him calculate how many pitchers of water there are in the sea and how many stars in the sky."

The king rose, he said to the rabbi: "Did you hear, oh rabbi?"

He said to him: "Yes, I hear."

He said to him: "Calculate how many pitchers of water there are in the sea and how many stars in the sky. If you succeed, the vizier's head will be cut off. If you don't, your head will be cut off, and the Jews of this country will be destroyed."

He said: "Give us forty days grace."

Our dear friend,[1] the rabbi, went to the congregation. They started praying the prayers of the Day of Atonement. Their world collapsed, for the king had issued this decree. The rabbi spent forty days with them.

On the thirty-ninth day there came a Jewish drunkard, who had not heard the news, he would murmur to himself. He found the Jews running here and there.

He asked them: "What happened? What's new?"

They said to him: "Haven't you heard? Is there nothing in your head?"

He said to them: "No, my head is empty."

They said to him: "The king has issued a decree [to the effect that] unless we tell him how many pitchers of water there are in the sea and how many stars in the sky, he will destroy us."

He said to them: "Is that all?"

They said to him: "That is all!"

He said to them: "Bring me a bottle of Arak, and I will tell you what to do."

Those who believed in him and relied on him said: "We do not know where the good is kept,[2] and perhaps some idea will occur to him."

Good. They brought him a bottle of Arak.

He said to them: "How much longer do we have?"

They said to him: "We have only one more day. If we do not bring him the calculation, the king will cut off our heads."

He said to them: "When you want to go, I am here, ready to go with you. Just bring me a bottle of Arak, let it be strong, and when it rises to my head, I will be your father."

They said to him: "Good."

They went with him; they went to the king.

When they arrived, they jumped to their feet and asked them: "What's new? Did you bring the calculation."

—"Yes, oh Sir."

The king said to him: "Where is the one who will answer . . . ?"

They said to him: "Here he is. Come here, oh drunkard."

---

[1] The words refer to the rabbi. They imply that the narrator identifies with him.

[2] That is, we do not know what, precisely, will save us.

He came before the king.

The king said to him: "Are you the one who wants to hand in the calculation?"

He said to him: "I am the one who is going to do the calculation. But promise me with your signature that if I give you the calculation, you will give me half the kingdom, and the vizier—his head will be cut off. And if not, you cut off my head and do with it whatever you like."

(Let's get on with the story, a law is a law . . . the poor Jews . . .)[3]

The king said to his vizier: "The person who will give you the answers is (standing) before you. What do you demand from the Jews?"

—"That they tell me how many pitchers of water there are in the sea and how many stars in the sky."

—"Well then," said the drunkard to the king, "give me your crown. Lift up your crown!"

The drunkard lifted up the crown and bared the king's head.

He said: "Look, as the number of hairs on your head so is the number of stars in the sky and the number of pitchers full of water in the sea."

The next day, they cut off the vizier's head and issued a proclamation in the land, announcing that the decree was canceled.

May you hear nothing but good things; there is no power like the power of the Jews.

## Commentary: IFA 16544

### THE KING, THE VIZIER, AND THE CLEVER JEW

The narrator heard this tale from poor people whom he used to invite to his house back in Morocco. He narrates it on various occasions. Shortly before we recorded it, he narrated it when he and members of the Jewish Burial Society were keeping watch at the bedside of a dying man. "It is our custom to sit with these people and to tell them stories, and I also narrated this tale," testifies Mordekhai Malka.

Typologically, this folktale belongs with the Jewish oicotype of Aarne-Thompson 922*C (IFA)—"Jews are forced by hostile minis-

---

[3] The narrator's remark indicates a break and identification.

ters of state to answer questions and to perform tasks,"[1] and it also links up with Aarne-Thompson *1703 (IFA)—"Jests and jokes about drunkards."[2]

The genre of this folktale is the novella of cleverness. It centers on a confrontation between two different religions and places the clever Jew and the vizier at the two poles, with the king serving as the neutral protagonist whom the two opponents try to win over by means of a display of cleverness and resourcefulness.

Tales about religious confrontations often develop into sacred legends; this happens when the holiness of the Jewish protagonist helps him resolve difficulties. In our tale, too, we expect at first that the resolution of the conflict is going to involve religion; the despondent Jews pray to God: they recite the prayers of the Day of Atonement to win the right to divine help. But the tale soon moves in a new direction: the rabbi, who was the protagonist and who had incurred the displeasure of the vizier, disappears. He is replaced by a different character, a Jewish drunkard who accomplishes the tasks and answers the questions.

The change of protagonists entails a change of situation: we move from the plane of gravity and rivalry between persons in high places to the plane of humor expressed through the drunkard and the way he relates to the Jewish community and the king and his Vizier. The fear verbalized by the prayers for the Day of Atonement abates when the drunkard appears and makes us laugh. He relates with disdain to the questions posed by the vizier, to which there is no answer, and relies on his bottle of arak. When he appears before the king, he is downright—and admirably—insolent, as only a drunkard can be.

There is no doubt that the development in the direction of the novella is triggered by the nature of the questions the vizier addresses to the Jew.[3] The questions are similar to those posed in Aarne-Thompson's international narrative type "The emperor and the abbot" (Aarne-Thompson 922), which centers on the confronta-

---

[1] This folktale has approximately seventy parallels in IFA. The following were printed: Noy 1964, nos. 49, 57, 62, 64; Avitsuk 1965, no. 11; Baharav 1964, no. 35; Nanah 1958–1976, pp. 172–182; Noy 1965, no. 88; Baharav 1968, nos. 2, 43; Noy 1965b, no. 33; Noy 1963a, no. 38; Yeshiva 1963, no. 5.

[2] Cf. also Va'yikra Raba 12, A; Gaster 1968, no. 305; Gaster 1934, no. 24; Ben-Yehezkel 1965, no. 327.

[3] This type of question occurs in many novellas; it is generally posed by someone wanting to put his spouse to the test, as for example in Aarne-Thompson 875 "The Clever Farmer's Daughter."

A certificate of a Shadar, a messenger of the Rabbis, Ksar Al Suk, 1912. By kind permission of the Israel Museum, Jerusalem.

tion between characters whose religion is identical but whose social class is different.

Anderson, who wrote an exhaustive monograph on the narrative type of the king who directs three questions to the abbot [4] ar-

---

[4] Cf. Anderson 1923.

gues that the origin of this type is Jewish. Other researchers contend that the narrative type originated in a Middle-Eastern Jewish community, possibly Egypt, early in the seventh century.[5]

Incidentally, in the Jewish-Yemenite[6] version in the IFA the Jewish opponent of the priest is again a drunkard, but sometimes the Jewish point of view is represented by a youth, so that the difference in faith is reinforced by the gap between the ages of the protagonists.

It appears that whenever the Jews are made to perform some task, such as discovering the answers to questions to which there is no answer, they are warned they will be severely punished if they fail to carry out the mission. In our narrative they are threatened with death: the rabbi's head will be cut off, and all the Jews will be put to death. However, in many Jewish versions the threat includes the national element of deportation to another country. Obviously, these tales are laid in countries of the Diaspora where Jews are oppressed. Our narrative combines the threat to the life of one individual (in the international folktale) with the antisemitic threat to the lives of all the Jews, which is subsequently reversed (in the Jewish version).

The solution, for which the protagonist resorts to a trick, is equally a feature of the many Jewish versions. A solution of this kind is also offered when the questions relate to a confrontation between the two religions. The question "which of the two religions is older?" is a case in point. To answer it, the Jew pulls a trick on those who are questioning him: he accuses them of stealing the shoes of Moses on Mt. Sinai. When they argue they have not been there, he uses their argument as the answer to the question asked by them.[7]

Incidentally, in some cases the international folktale type of the emperor and the abbot has linkages with the humorous tale, for example, "doctor know-all" (Aarne-Thompson 1641). This type is named after the hero in the German versions, who may be a con-man, a quack and so on, who manages to guess the name of the animal or the object the interrogator had in mind.

---

[5] Cf. Yeshiva 1963, note to no. 5.

[6] IFA 69, narrated by Yefet Schwili, recorded by Heda Jason (Noy 1965, no. 88).

[7] Cf. Seri 1978, note to no. 7.

# Freḥa Ḥafutah

**WHEN THE** folktales were recorded, Freḥa Ḥafutah was about ninety years old. Her father's name was Shlomo Malul, and her mother's name was Zohara. They lived in Bejo, in the Atlas Mountains, and with their daughters they wandered to the Moroccan towns of Derey, Ka'ala, and Casablanca.

She and her four children came to Israel in 1955, and when we recorded her, she was living in Shlomi with her daughter Sultana.

She never had a job and was always at home, and she had no formal education. When she was a child in her native land, she heard many folk narratives, mainly from her family. When we recorded her, she said she no longer heard people tell folk narratives; perhaps the reason was that she was blind and could no longer go out. She herself continued to offer folk narratives at home. But according to her testimony, people cared less for her narratives than they had previously.

# Smeda Rmeda

### FROM: FREḤA ḤAFUTA

Let me tell you, God was everywhere, but he was in our hands and in the listeners' hands. Our house is silk and cotton, but the house of the Muslims will be ruined and all the Muslims will be destroyed in a single day.

There was, let me tell you, a certain woman. She had just one son and one daughter—that was all she had in the whole world. The girl used to go out with her girl friends every day: she went to school with them, combed her hair with them, and played and laughed with them.

One of God's fine days the neighbor—the mother of the girls—said to her: "Listen, why are you always hanging around my daughters? Your mother does not pay any attention to you, and does not love you, and does nothing for you. You must kill her."

She said to her: "How do you want me to kill my mother. What for?"

She said to her: "What should you do? Get a snake and put it in the butter jar." (Let's get on with the story, dear friends.[1]) So the girl said to her: "How am I to kill my mother?"

She said to her: "Get the snake and put it in the butter jar and pretend you are sick and go to sleep, and tell her: 'Mother, cook a little Barkuksh for me.'"[2]

"And when she says: 'Rise, oh her brother, go and get the butter,' tell her: 'His hands are not clean.'

—'Rise, oh her father, go.'

"Tell her: 'His hands are hairy.'

—'Rise, oh the servant, go.'

"Tell her: 'Her hands are black. Mother, you go.'

And when she goes and gets the butter, she dies. And then your father will come and ask me to be his wife, and you will be the dearest person in the whole world to me."

Good. This is what the poor girl did. She went to her mother and told her: "I am not going to school today."

---

[1] The narrator is addressing the women to whom she is telling the tale.

[2] The dish is cooked with semolina and milk and served with butter.

—"Why, my daughter?"

—"I am sick, mother, sick."

She said to her: "My daughter, what can I do for you?"

She said to her: "I want to sleep."

She slept. And the poor mother made her bed lovingly and put her to bed.

—"I am your Kappara,"[3] she said. "What can I do to help you?"

She said to her: "Just cook a little Barkuksh for me."

And she had already put the viper into the opening of the butter jar—may God spare us such misfortune.

The daughter was asleep, and the mother wanted to cook some Barkuksh for her.

—"Rise, oh her brother. Go and get the butter."

She said to him: "Your hands are dirty."

—"Rise, oh the servant, and go."

—"Her hands are black."

—"Rise, oh her father, and go."

—"No, father's hands are hairy. Mother, you go. Wash your hands."

Good. She got up from her chair, washed her hands, the poor woman—May you not see misfortune. The moment she stepped into that cursed cellar to get the butter the viper attacked her. The mother died; may you not see misfortune, and may you not see evil. She died, the poor woman.

Good, seven days went by, eight days, time went by.

Now don't you say anything![4] One day the girl rose and went out with the daughters of the neighbor as usual: she goes out with them, washes, takes a shower, and gets dressed.

She said to her: "Now that your father is alone with you and your brother, go and tell him, tell your father to marry me, and you will be the dearest person in the world to me."

Good, she went to her father, and said to him: "Father, the kind of life we are leading is not good. Will you remain without a wife? There is our neighbor whom we love and who is a close friend. Marry her, and she will take care of us."

He said to her: "Oh my daughter, there is time for a wedding."

She implored him, the poor girl, and he married her. He married the neighbor.

Now don't you say anything! What did her seven daughters do?

---

[3] Kappara means expiatory sacrifice. "I am prepared to let my life be an expiatory sacrifice for you" (an expression of love).

[4] The phrase is a typical connector.

They stood above the father's beard, her father, and relieved themselves, if you will excuse me. They soiled his beard and his clothes.

The poor man rose: "Oh my God, who did this to me?"

She said to him: "I weep for you and your daughter (excuse me),[5] yes, she is the one that did what she wanted to do."

—"By God, my daughter would never do such a thing, neither she nor her brother. Don't you dare to say a thing like that."

She said to him: "What can we do to her? Let's lock her up in the baking room for the night, and you will see what she does."

They grabbed her and locked her up there for the night. The next morning, the father woke up in the same state as before, and they did this to him day after day.

The girls would climb up to the opening in the roof, above the baking room, and they would do it.

The neighbors protested: "By God, oh my daughter, do you think there is something wrong with the daughter of your husband? She leaves the baking room, relieves herself and goes back. And they lock her up in the room, the poor girl."

Don't you say anything, my dear friends! Time passes, and the king's son announces that he is looking for a wife.

Nobody stayed indoors, not even drummers, buglers, or people who scour their faces with red-hot loam.[6]

Don't you say anything, my dear! The father of the unlucky girl who was locked in the room where the oven was, wanted to go to Marrakesh.

The girls said to him: "Bring me a kerchief."

And another girl said: "A pair of slippers."

And another: "A dress."

He rose and said to his wife: "Oh my daughter, I will go to the orphan and ask her, too, what she wants."

—"Sit down, sit down," she told him. "You just sit down. She is covered all over with soot and excrement; you have no reason to go and ask her."

He said to her: "No. I will go to her, poor girl that she is."

He went to the baking room; he said to her: "I am going to Marrakesh to do some shopping. The king's son is looking for a wife, and my wife's daughters have told me what they want me to buy for them. Now what do you want me to buy for you? "

She said to him: "Father, just bring me seven nuts."

---

[5] The narrator apologizes for being rude.

[6] That is to say, the whole population came, even the poorest and the ugliest.

He said to her: "Very good, oh my daughter."

Good, he went to Marrakesh, and he bought ever so many things, but he forgot all about the seven nuts, the poor fellow. On the way home he remembered and went back to Marrakesh. What did he buy? He bought a sack full of nuts. But the sack had a hole, and as he was walking the nuts fell to the ground, until there were only seven nuts left.

He returned; he brought her the nuts. He said to her: "Daughter, take these nuts. They are what God and your luck gave you. I brought you a sack, my daughter, and now . . ."

She said to him: "Father, give them to me. These seven nuts are enough to bring me luck—God will give me luck."

Good. She took the seven nuts and hid them.

The king was getting married. The step-mother—may you be spared such calamities—gathered together all kinds of grain and kernels—barley, wheat, corn—everything, mixed them in one room and climbed up to the attic.

She said to her: "If you don't sort these out and put each grain where it belongs, I'll give you short shrift."

She sent the girl to that room. The girl cried—the moment she wiped one eye, the other eye started getting wet.

She cracked the first nut. The nut was empty.

She cracked the second nut. Samsam-Kamkam[7] came out. When the demon came out, her luck appeared.

—"Whatever you wish, my Lady—it will be done."

She said to him: "You see what a fix I am in, don't you?"

Good, he worked, sorting out everything. This goes here, in this sack, and that goes there, in that sack, and again in that sack. He sewed up the sacks, and the room was spotless. Then he left and disappeared.

The poor girl cracked the third nut. Someone appeared—his horse was green, his headgear was green, his dress was green and his sword was green to match. He said to her: "Everything my Lady wants done will be done."

She said to him: "What my Lady wants done will be done?— She wants to be taken from here to the king's wedding feast."

He took her, he carried her and turned her into a charming girl (may God grant you this without a story and without a tale. May He grant you luck and may your husbands live.)[8] He turned her into a

---

[7] A gigantic demon usually described as "having its head in the sky and his feet in the water." Some people call it Samsam ben Kamkam.

[8] The narrator blesses the listeners.

beautiful girl, carried her on his shoulders to the wedding feast of the king's son.

The girls are talking, and one of them says: "Mother, mother, mother, there is our sister. Here she comes."

The mother said to her: "Be quiet. That is the king's daughter." That is what the step-mother—may you be spared such a calamity—says. "This," she says, "is a princess, that poor girl is locked up in a dark room."

Good. The people laugh and eat and drink. They laid a regal table for the girl, and she sits down, eats, drinks in the king's house, the house of the wedding.

Good. The wedding feast is over, and the people left, and only she stayed. She cracked the first nut, found it was rotten, the second was rotten, until she got to the last nut, the seventh. She cracked it, and someone on horseback appeared—the horse was red; the head dress was red to match.

—"Whatever my Lady wants done will be done!"

—"She wants to be taken away now, and she wants to be put in the baking room where her father's wife put her."

And the room is swept clean and there is nothing in it.

On her way back she lost one shoe. No other girl had a shoe like that, and who should find it but the king's son who was looking for a wife.

He said: "There is only one person whom this shoe will fit."

All the girls living in that country were brought to him—all of them. The shoe was too large for one girl, too small for another.

They rose and said: "We tried them all. There is only one girl left; she is hidden in a baking room.

He said to them: "Fetch her."

The mother said to him: "This ought not to be done, sir. She is covered with excrement and soot, and what is she to be fetched for?"

He said to them: "Get her, no matter what."

They brought her before him. He put the beautiful shoe on her foot, and it was a perfect fit.

He said to her: "You are the one I am going to marry."

—"Sir, she does not suit you . . ."

He said to her: "This is the one I want."

Good, the servant girls carried her to the bath-house, gave her a dress that suited her, took her, bathed her, dressed her, and took her to the king's son.

He made a big wedding feast, and only God is great, may God grant you and us such a feast.

Don't you say anything! The cursed woman, the father's wife, envied the girl. What did she do? The girl became pregnant; she was in an advanced stage of pregnancy, the poor girl.

Don't you say anything! The father's wife rose and said to her daughters: "Rise, come, let us go and visit your sister and see what God has given her."

(Envy!)[9]

Don't you say anything! They went to see her; they checked them over and let them in.

The people said: "Her father's wife and her daughters?"[10]

Good, the king's son let them in.

These women sit and say: "Come and we'll take you for a walk and cheer you up . . ."

They took her for a walk, and when they came to a well they threw her into it. In this well there lived lions and demons. They threw her into the well, and she fell onto the back of a lioness.

What did the sisters do? What did the mother do? She took her daughter, the one who was blind in one eye, put make-up on her face, dressed her, and sent her to the king's son.

The king's son came and talked to her, but she would not answer.

He said to her: "What happened to your eye?"

She said to him: "What happened to my eye? My brother grabbed me and gouged it out."

He said to her: "And what do you want me to do to your brother?"

She said to him: "What do I want you to do to him? Let's slaughter him, put him into a loaf of bread and send him to our home."

He said to her: "All right, oh my daughter."

And the poor brother heard everything. He went to that well, weeping, the poor boy.

He said to her:

My sister, oh my sister,
Oh daughter of our father and mother,
The ovens are heating up
And the knives are being sharpened.

The poor girl rose and replied:

---

[9] The narrator's aside.

[10] Irony.

My brother, oh my brother,
Oh son of our father and mother,
I am caught between the lion and the lioness,
And the king's sleeve is in my hands
And the daughters of the women have betrayed me.

(When I tell this tale, my tears flow. It is heart-rending.)[11]

Good, the king's son passed by and found the boy sitting next to the well, weeping, pleading with her, listening to her [tale of woe].

He said to him: "Say that again, my child. Repeat what you were saying. Say it again!" He sat there and said to her:

My sister, oh my sister,
Oh daughter of my father and mother,
The knives have been sharpened,
And the ovens are heating up.

And she rises and replies:

My brother, oh my brother,
Oh son of our father and mother,
I am caught between the lion and the lioness
And the sleeve of the king's son is in my hands
And the daughters of the woman have set me a trap.

Don't you say anything, my dear! He said to him: "Nice."

He went to the magicians, to the greatest of them and said to him: "Oh master, a boy beside the well is beseeching someone, and somebody answers him from inside the well, and I do not know who it is."

And the one-eyed one, her mother left her behind, she is hiding in the palace and does not want to talk to him.

The chief magician said to him: "Go ahead and slaughter seven oxen, slaughter them and throw them down that well."

Good. They did so.

—"Oh, who did us this favor? Who did us this favor? We'll return it."

The girl appeared; she got off the lioness' back and is holding the child.

She had given birth inside the well, the poor girl, inside the well.

She climbed from the well, holding her child, and the king's son grabbed her.

—"Oh my daughter, who did this?"

---

[11] The narrator's aside.

She said to him: "Come, come, come, and be silent. The knives that were sharpened for my brother (may I never see such a thing happen to my brothers)[12] and the ovens that are heating up will be heated up for the one-eyed girl, and she will be sent to our house in a sack."

Good. He took her; he took the poor girl of whom the women said: "Smeda Rmeda who destroyed her good fortune with her own hands."

Don't you say anything! This is what they did: They brought the blind girl, policemen took her, slaughtered her and cut her up, and they lit the bread oven and the meat oven, they took the blind head and hid it and put chunks of flesh in layers between some bread, and put it on a lame she-ass's back, and told the she-ass: "Go. Come back the way you started out."

—"Hurrah," the mother rejoiced, "her daughter sent her a present, her daughter sent her a present. She feels good."

She took the sack, and gave everybody some bread and a piece of meat.

—"Here you are. Take some."

Don't you say anything, my dear friends—till she got to the head and recognized her daughter's head. Then she wailed: "All those who have shared bread with me—come and shed tears with me." (May God give you luck, and may your children and your husbands live).[13]

The girl was lucky, and they made a big wedding feast, but only God is great.

> And the tale floats on the rivers
> And you, my friends, are cheerful givers.

Seven apples appeared, you ate one and another [woman] ate one, and yet another ate one, and Abraham took what was left. Good, I left Abraham out, perhaps he married her.

---

[12] Narrator's aside.

[13] The narrator blesses the audience.

## Commentary: IFA 16446

### SMEDA RMEDA

This is a Moroccan-Jewish version of Cinderella (Aarne-Thompson 510).[1] According to the testimony of the narrator, her mother used to tell it to her children before they went to sleep. The purpose of the tale was to teach them to love their mother, to keep away from strange women trying to interfere in the affairs of the family, and to give preference to their own family over their boy friends and girl friends.

The majority of Jewish versions of the Cinderella narrative type, as well as the present tale, link up with the Jewish oicotype of matricide—Aarne-Thompson 510*D (IFA)[2]—featuring the motif of murder at the direction of an evil neighbor who incites a daughter to kill her mother.

In the manner of the Maerchen, our tale deals with powerful urges that clash with one another. But feelings are not verbalized in the folktale; they are expressed through deeds, and consequently terrible things happen that witness the violent drives underlying them. This led to the formation of this genre: the daughter causes her mother's death, the sister in disguise is slaughtered and cut up limb by limb, the mother eats the flesh of her daughter, and so on.[3]

Bruno Bettelheim, the psychologist who "legitimized" children's fairy tales (Bettelheim 1980), thinks that beneath the overt content of the Cinderella story hides a confusion of complex and often unconscious material. For example, a child who believes that parents and siblings treat the child very badly and that this suffering is unbearable will discover that the fate of the heroine is infinitely worse than his or her own. The story tells him therefore that he or she is lucky and that things might be much worse. But the happy ending of the fairy tale calms fears as to the other possibility.

Bettelheim thinks that, beneath the conscious plain on which Cinderella's troubles are caused by the wickedness of her step-

---

[1] For an exhaustive study of this type, see Cox 1893; Rooth 1951. Twenty-five parallel versions are in IFA: Morocco (8), Tunis(2), Turkey (1), Lebanon (1), Israel Sefardi (1), Yemen (2), Iraqi Kurdistan (2), Persian Kurdistan (2), Iraq (1), Bukhara (3), Afghanistan (1), Rumania (1).

[2] Five parallel versions are in IFA: Morocco (2), Yemen (1), Persian Kurdistan (2).

[3] The punishment meted out to the step-mother and her daughter is usually very cruel. Cf., e.g., Noy 1966, no. 67.

A bottle for rose water, Rabat, the middle of the twentieth century. By kind permission of the Israel Museum, Jerusalem.

mother and sisters, there is the subconscious plain disguised in the versions of the story current today. In his view, the misery of the heroine results from her Oedipal desire, and her innocence is Oedipal guilt in disguise. At the end of the Oedipal period, the child's feelings of guilt caused by a wish to be dirty and untidy combine with Oedipal guilt feelings resulting from a wish to occupy the place of the same sex parent in the affections of the other parent. The wish to be loved by the opposite sex parent, and perhaps even to be a sex partner, looks natural and "innocent" at first, but at the end of this period it is repressed as a wicked wish. Although the child represses the wish itself, the child does not repress the feelings of guilt attached to it and consequently feels dirty and worthless.

In this story, the desire clearly materializes: the daughter kills her mother, and consequently the punishment seems just. She is humiliated, rejected, hated, and isolated in the baking room where soot and dirt cover her from head to foot.

In the European versions of the tale the girl is imprisoned in the fireplace, which, according to Bettelheim, is a mother symbol. The close proximity to the fireplace, with the girl actually sitting in the ashes (or in the soot), therefore symbolizes the attempt to hold on to the mother or to return to her and what she stands for. Thus the heroine mourns not only the loss of her real mother but also the loss of her dreams of a relationship with her father-lover. When the daughter, according to Bettelheim's reading, overcomes her great Oedipal disappointment, she is no longer a child, but a mature young woman ready for marriage, and thus she can return to a successful life as the tale draws to a close.

However, it is possible to link the girl in the ashes or in the baking room (from which the title of the protagonist in the European versions derives)[4] to fire and its symbolism: fire does not only burn (as the fireplace or baking room does not stand for dirt only), but it purges, cleanses, and purifies. The vestal virgins in Greek mythology, for instance, guarded the fire so it should never die, and they were the hallmark of perfect purity. Only after they had successfully accomplished the task did they win the right to a prestigious marriage (as did Cinderella), which shows that innocence, purity, and guarding the fire were connected in ancient cultures.

The breach of norms that constitutes a societal taboo is a characteristic feature of this tale. Breaking the norms is part of the essence of the fairy tale; as the mask worn by the actor on the Greek stage freed him from the dangers posed by breaking a taboo, so the "not here and not now" in which the fairy tale is laid enables the narrator to override taboos without being at risk whilst causing the listeners to experience catharsis.

However, the narrator is aware of the feelings of anxiety that the events described may stir up in the listeners and perhaps in herself too, and she takes several precautionary measures to "soften" their impact:

1. Whenever frightening matters are referred to, the narrator is careful to point out that both the listeners and she herself are excluded. For example: "She had already placed the snake in the opening of the jar—may your lives be spared." And when we are told that knives are being sharpened in preparation of the slaughter of Smeda Rmeda's brother, she hastens to add: "May my brother's life be spared."
2. As soon as acts of cruelty are mentioned, the narrator hastens to bless the listeners. When the mother realizes that she has eaten her own daughter, she starts wailing; at this point the narrator

---

[4] The French name Cendrillou derives from the word *cender*, or ashes. The German Aschenputtel equally stresses the fact that the heroine lives where the ashes are. According to Bruno Bettelheim, the English translation is faulty, as the correct translation is *ashes* not *cinder*. We could not trace the name *Smeda Rmeda* in written sources, but according to the story tellers in Judeo Arabic it suggests semolina flour (Smeda) and ashes (rmeda).

quickly turns to the listeners: "May God give you luck, and may your children live and may your husbands live."
3. Whenever someone blesses a character in the tale, the narrator points out that the listeners are equally blessed.

Undoubtedly, "softening" the events narrated reflects a cultural trait of a narrating society that attaches magic power to the spoken word. A study of the tale moreover indicates that the cultural changes resulting from the absorption of Israeli culture have left their impact on the Jewish-Moroccan folktale.

In the tale, a proverb is quoted: "Smeda Rmeda who destroyed her luck with her own hands." This is a Jewish-Moroccan proverb commonly used to describe a person who does a well-intentioned disservice to himself.

There seems to be no doubt that the proverb originated from this tale, which proves its wide distribution among Moroccan Jews. The proverb is still in use, and the second generation of Moroccan Jews in Israel know it, but when we conducted an investigation on a limited scale we found that the story is not known to them.[5] This implies that a short saying that does not conflict with present-day culture remains in everyday speech, but families no longer find time to sit down together and tell folktales that move at a leisurely pace and presuppose a certain relaxed frame of mind.

The fabulous creatures that populate the tale are another cultural trait. As we know, the man-world relation embedded in the tale is fabulous, and fabulous creatures set the tale in motion; they operate in the world of human beings and help the protagonist in his/her struggle against his/her enemies. Even though the task imposed by the step-mother on the girl is identical with the task required by the European fairy tale, the fabulous creature coming to the rescue in our tale is not a fairy but Samsam-Kamkam, a Middle-Eastern fabulous creature usually described with "his head is in the sky and his feet are in the water," or in similar terms.

The motif involving a prohibition (the protagonists may not stay beyond a certain point of time—Motif C 761.3), which is a feature of this narrative type, is absent from this tale, but the shoe test is the same as that in the international narrative type.

Incidentally, the small foot unrivaled in size is a treasured pos-

---

[5] We are indebted to Ms. Penina Peri, an Israeli of Moroccan descent who transcribed the tale for us. When Ms. Peri told us that the tale had helped her understand why her mother used to quote this saying, we followed up her remark and decided to investigate the subject with a larger group of second-generation Moroccan Jews living in Israel.

session, and the material used to make the shoe is hard to find; these details seem to suggest Eastern or perhaps Chinese origins. Listeners in the Middle East do not associate sexual attraction and beauty with unusually small feet, as the Chinese used to do (which explains the Chinese custom of binding the feet of girls), and sometimes another object, such as a ring, stands in for the shoe.

According to the approach taken by folklore researchers of the psychoanalytic school, the shoe is a distinctly female symbol: it is a small receptacle which can be penetrated by a part of the body which fits it exactly. The shoe can symbolize the vagina; also, it may be an object easily lost at the end of a party, and hence it is an image of virginity. The prince searching the father's house parallels the bridegroom asking for the girl's hand in marriage. In our version of the tale, the prince puts the shoe on the girl's foot by himself; this may be compared to the bridegroom putting the ring on the bride's finger as part of the wedding ceremony.

Thus the narrative conflict is practically resolved, but now it transpires that this is no more than a temporary solution. The aggressiveness of the step-mother and her daughters escalates as the plot unfolds, and the baking room is replaced by the well into which the heroine is thrown. The second part of the plot is therefore an escalating repetition of the first part, and it is obvious that a happy ending would be incomplete without punishing the opponents.

We should note several characteristic features of the narrator's art: when the brother addresses his sister down the well he sings in verse, and so does she when she replies. This performance device combines with the narrator's verbal art to ask for the listeners' attention.

Moreover, the narrator is in the habit of placing a dividing line between the various episodes. To do so, she marks time: "Good, seven days went by, eight days went by, time went by," or again "Time goes by and time comes." Thus she creates intervals that permit the listeners to relate to each episode as a whole.

The opening sentences used by the narrator are features of the Jewish-Moroccan folktale. To begin, the fundamental sanctity of God is established; next, the listeners are allowed to share the secret of the tale with the narrator: "Our house is all silk and cotton, and the Muslims' house will be demolished and all the Muslims be destroyed in one day." The sentence expresses the feelings of the listeners—their hatred of an oppressive majority.

The conclusion is equally a feature of the Jewish-Moroccan folktale. It returns the listeners to the real world. The apple is the fictitious gift given to the listeners by the narrator. Abraham, who is being referred to as the person receiving the apples that are left over, is a listener as well as the boy friend of the narrator's daughter. Undoubtedly the conclusion serves to convey the narrator's wishes regarding their relationship, and thus we see again that the tale is a social act of reciprocity allowing a message to be transmitted, which for various reasons cannot perhaps be conveyed directly.

# My Sister Mass'uda and My Brother Mass'ud

FROM: FREḤA ḤAFUTA

A certain man had seven daughters and a wife. The luckless man, whatever he brought home in the daytime he would eat at night. One day he did not find anything to eat and he did not find anything to bring his daughters.

He said: "Bless God, I will go into the wilderness. If I don't die, I will live.

Good, he walked, walked in the wilderness till he came to a certain place, and there he sat down at night.

There came Mother Ghula[1] and her seven children. She ran, da-da, da-da; she was happy that God had provided a supper for her. He fell upon her, embraced her: "Mass'uda, my sister."

—"Mass'ud my brother."

—"Mass'uda my sister, welcome!"

—"Welcome, Mass'ud my brother, welcome! Do you have any sons? Do you have any daughters?"

He said to her: "I have seven daughters and a wife. And I did not find anything to eat for them."

Good.

She said to him: "Close your eyes and open them."

He opened his eyes and found himself beneath the ground. There he found things, God may bless you and us, without a story

---

[1] A demon that eats human beings; see commentary.

and without a tale, may God give you just that, everything is full of gold and silver, unlike any other place.

There he stays, eats, drinks; each day she slaughters a sheep for him; she slaughters each day. She fattens him up in order to eat him.

He said to her: "Oh my daughter, do not eat me. I have seven daughters."

She said to him: "Good, if you have seven daughters, take these seven horses laden with money, take them and bring your daughters and your wife and come."

He said to her: "Good."

(Woe be to you, you unfortunate man, you took seven horses laden with money, go and stay at home.)[2]

He said to his wife: "Rise, rise, come on now. I found a certain woman, Mass'uda, my sister, who will gladden your heart."

—"A certain Mass'uda, my sister?! You unfortunate man, Mass'uda, your sister, from what place did she come to you?" He said to her: "Come on, rise, come on now, may your father's house be laid waste. Come on now, God has given us a place to live."
She said to him: "Woe be to you."

Good. He took the money and hid it in the backyard. The fool, he took his daughters and his wife and walked, walked, walked up to the entrance of the pit. It was night.

One of the daughters said: "Mother, oh mother, where is she, where is Mass'uda? Where is my Aunt Mass'uda about whom our father told me?"

She said to her: "Be quiet, oh my daughter, for your father brought you here to die. And now I am going to pull a trick on him; don't you be afraid."

Well, they sit there, and they sit there, and suddenly he jumps to his feet: "Mass'uda, my sister."

—"Mass'ud, my brother, Mass'ud, my brother."

The mother said to her daughters: "Woe to us."

—"Oh mother, is this the aunt to whom my father took us?"

They went beneath the ground. They sit; they eat and drink.

She said to the mother: "Now give me one of your daughters, I want her to sleep in my room."

She took her first daughter, the wretched creature, she took her and said to her: "Take her."

She gave her needles.

She said to her: "Clean my teeth. If you don't, I'll eat you."

She started cleaning her teeth. She cleans, and she cleans, and

---

[2] The narrator's aside to the hero.

she cleans, and she cleans, and she trembles with fear, the poor girl.

The next morning, the girl said: "Mother, oh mother, this aunt bared her enormous teeth;[3] she told me to clean them, and if I didn't, she would eat me."

This is how the first night passed.

The second night she said to the mother: "Give me your second daughter."

She gave her her second daughter.

She brought her combs. She said to her: "Take them. Comb my hair, and if you don't I'll kill you."

The girl said [to herself]: Woe unto me.

The second daughter too got through the night.

The third night she said to the third daughter: "Take my clothes, and delouse them, and if you don't, I'll eat you."

The third daughter stayed with her and deloused her clothes.

In this way, she made all the seven girls do some work for her. One cleaned her feet, another cleaned her head, another cleaned her teeth, and so on. Till she had forced all of them to spend the night in her room. And that is how, for a month, the poor girls lay in bed trembling with fear.

One [of the girls] said to the mother: "Is that what father brought us here for?"

She said to her: "Be quiet, oh my daughter."

The Ghula said to the mother: "And now you listen to what I am going to tell you: give your daughters to my sons in marriage. You have seven daughters, and I have seven sons; let them get married!"

What did she do to her? She said to her: "It is our custom to make the girls wear kerchiefs and the boys hats."

She said to her: "Good."

They did so.

She [the mother] said to her: "Tell me, oh my sister-in-law, how do you sleep?"

She said to her: "When I have eaten my fill, I close my eyes, and I open my mouth when I am asleep; and when I am hungry I open my eyes, and I close my mouth when I am asleep."

She said to her: "Good, thank you for telling me."

What did Mass'ud's wife do? She took the kerchiefs, gave them to the boys, and made her seven daughters put on the hats.

What did she do? She waited till Ghula had eaten her fill and

---

[3] At this point, the narrator demonstrates the size of the teeth using special intonation and gestures.

95

Amulet hangers with writing. Tarodanat. By kind permission of the Israel Museum, Jerusalem.

opened her mouth and closed her eyes. Mass'ud's wife took her daughters and removed them one by one, one by one.

She put money on the backs of seven horses, led them out into the open and left, slowly but surely. And 'Mass'ud, my brother'— she left him there, asleep in a corner.

(Serves him right.)[4]

The foolish Mother Ghula rose, found the kerchiefs. What did she do? She got hold of those who were wearing those kerchiefs. She ate her seven children, she ate, and she ate, and she ate, and she ate, and she ate, and she ate, and she ate till she had eaten all of them, and there was nothing left; then she left the room in order to look for the wife of 'Mass'ud, my brother.'

The woman said to her: "Oh Mother Ghula, you meant to pull a trick on me, but I pulled a trick on you. You see, you ate your sons, and my daughters are right here next to me."

Good. Mother Ghula left, she ran, and ran, and ran, and ran, and ran, and ran, and ran, and found her brother Mass'ud.

—"Mass'ud my brother, my brother Mass'ud, where do I start eating you?"

He said to her: "Start with my ears because I didn't listen to my wife's advice."

She fell upon him, she eats, eats, eats until she has eaten him. She left, ran, ran, ran, until she left nothing but bones, and she threw herself into the river. And these Ghulas, when there is a river they cannot cross it. She fell into the river and died.

Mass'ud's wife said: "Go, and may you not be brought back to life."

Mass'ud's wife went to the king, she said to him: "Rise, and I will make you and your soldiers rich."

She took the king's soldiers and went to that place. She gathered God's good things, may you and we [do the same] without any story or tale. She took the money and took, forgive me for saying so, 'Mass'ud, my brother' and put him into a sack.

She took all the money and left nothing beneath the ground.

Mother Ghula was dead, and her seven sons were dead, may God spare you, and Mass'ud's wife took her daughters and the money and made the king rich.

So may God give you and us [riches] without a story and without a tale.

---

4 Narrator's aside.

## *Commentary:* IFA 16445

### MY SISTER MASS'UDA AND MY BROTHER MASS'UD

This folktale belongs to the type "Man-Monster Partnership" (Aarne-Thompson 1030–1059). A man makes a deal with a monster, the monster proves to be a fool, and the man has the best of it. The genre is the fabulous tale. The Ghula, which is also known to the Arabs of Morocco (Westermark 1968, 369–400) is a fabulous monster; it is different from the demons in which Moroccan Jews believe. The belief in demons stems from Jewish sources dating back to the times of the Mishna (200 A.D.) and the Talmud (500 A.D.), as well as to the period when the Kabbala began to take shape.[1] The Ghula (also Ghula for the ancient Arabs) was a peculiarly bestial, diabolic, and hostile variety of the marids of the djinn that lured men off their path by assuming different forms, then fell upon them unawares, destroyed, and devoured them. In folklore it was an ordinary word for cannibal, whether human or demonic and thus became equivalent to the European ogre.[2]

To meet with the fabulous creature, man must leave human space and move to another space that in folk literature appears to be intermediate and that is inhabited by fabulous creatures rather than men. In this tale, as well as in many similar tales, the intermediate space is a wasteland, and the time to meet with the fabulous creatures is a charged time, that is, night.

The protagonist, who leaves his home in search of a fabulous creature ready to help him is by definition a luckless man who cannot provide for his family so that a change for the better on the lines of the maxim "Change of place—change of fortune"[3] is not to be expected. The fabulous creature he is fated to meet is the man-eating predator Ghula who lives on the flesh of humans. It has enormous protruding teeth and hair that needs constant combing; moreover, its gait is peculiar and its sleep patterns strange. There is an aura of terror about it; yet it is comic—the way it walks is ludicrous. Although it is stronger than man, it needs his services; man is shown to be more clever and hence able to outwit it. This reflects man's secret wish to use his cunning and resourcefulness to defeat

---

[1] Cf. Ben-Ami 1976a, 165–170.

[2] Cf. *The Encyclopedia of Islam* (1924) 3: 165–166.

[3] I.e., if an unlucky man moves to a new neighborhood or a different country, he may well be lucky there.

greater and stronger forces;[4] humans are too weak physically to stand a chance in their encounter with stronger creatures. The tactics of deceit, which the weak must use to defend themselves, are held legitimate by the narrating society. The narrative type "The Heavy Axe" (Aarne-Thompson 1049)[5] is a case in point. A sly braggart is told to fell trees or to carry water. To strike terror into the monster, he asks for a giant bucket to carry all the water in the spring, and a giant axe to fell all the trees in the forest.

Sometimes, the supernatural creature stands for evasion, for a kind of censorship that hides an overlord, a taskmaster, and so on.

The fairy tale typically features a protagonist who closes his eyes in order to move from one space to another. The Ghula typically resides underground: here, there are treasures of gold and silver. The popular belief that treasures are hidden underground (Motif F 721.4) and that they can only be accessed by fabulous monsters who guard them is familiar; this belief is mainly held in mining districts where these creatures were literally believed to act as guardians of treasure.[6]

To take possession of the treasures man had to outwit a monster, which is what happens in this story.

---

[4] Cf., e.g., Fallah and Shenhar 1978, no. 26, and note.

[5] Three versions are recorded in IFA. They are from Tunisia, Turkey and Israel. (For the Druze, see Fallah and Shenhar, ibid.)

[6] Cf., e.g., Widra 1973, 48–56.

# RABBI ḤANANIA PORTAL

RABBI PORTAL was born in 1917 in the town of Mugadur (Suera) in Morocco. He was married in 1944, and a year later his only son was born.

He was educated at a Talmud-Tora school and a Yeshiva and then served as a teacher in a Talmud-Tora school in Morocco.

As a child his mother told him folk narratives. When he grew up, he listened to the narratives presented by neighbors and old people. Nowadays, he no longer listens to folk narratives; instead, he reads collections of legends in either Hebrew or Judeo-Moroccan. He likes telling stories, and he continues narrating folk narratives. By narrating in the synagogues he combines it with a sermon. Moreover, he narrates in the appropriate setting "when an example must be given." He thinks the best time for story telling is the Sabbath and the holidays, and according to him people care for his stories and ask him to tell them.

The narrator speaks Hebrew fluently, and thus he preferred narrating his narratives in Hebrew, as opposed to the other narrators who narrated in Judeo-Arabic.

# The Miracle that Occurred between Purim and Pessah

FROM: RABBI ḤANANIA PORTAL

There were two brothers. One was rich, and the other was poor. The poor brother's children were all boys. God only gave him sons. The rich brother's children were all girls. He had nothing but daughters. That's the way it was. The poor brother was really very, very poor, as poor as poor can be. Whenever another child was born to him, he would go to his rich brother and ask him to give him something.

In those days the government did not help.[1] Everybody had to fend for himself and make do with what he had.

He would go to his brother. Each time another child was born, he would go to his brother. But his brother would turn him away. He would say: "I don't have anything. Go away." And he would give him nothing.

When he had several small children, and God was about to give him another child, he again went to his brother and said to him: "I want you to know that it is very cold, and I have nothing to keep my children and my wife warm, and we are destitute."

—"Look here," he said to him. "Me? I have nothing. I cannot give you anything." The poor man left, weeping. But before he came home, the Heavens opened for him, and God sent help.

Someone walked up to him, and he said to him: "Look here, brother, let me give you a piece of advice. This is what you should do."

He replied: "Yes. What?"

The man said: "Tomorrow you go to the market, and you buy a kuskus[2] dish, and spread a nice cloth on top of it. Take that to the king. Put it on the king's head, and he will give you all you need."

---

[1] The narrator contrasts the conditions in Morocco with the new realities of life in Israel; see commentary.

[2] Kuskus is a North African Jewish dish prepared with semolina. It is the basis of the food of the people throughout northwest Africa, both Muslims and Jews. To make Kuskus special dishes are used: a wooden dish called *djafna* or *ksa'a* to roll the semolina, a *kedra* that is a kind of earthenware saucepan; and a *keskas* that is a

In those days these dishes were made of clay. They made them of clay. In the Holy Language [Hebrew], we say "pottery."

He said to him: "Take it to the king. Tell him you brought him a nice present. When all his friends are sitting there together with him, put it on his head."

The man did not know what to do. What should he do? He spoke to his wife, and he told her everything. She said to him: "Perhaps this was the prophet Elijah. Perhaps you should buy what he told you to buy. Perhaps what he suggested is right."

So the man bought the dish, and as he was making the purchase everybody saw him. He went home, took a nice cloth, spread it on top of the dish, and went to the king. There was a guard at the door, and the man said to the guard: "Would you mind opening the door? The king . . . I want to see the king. I brought him a gift."

Good. The guard spoke to the king. He said: "There is a poor Jew at the door. He says he wants to give you a present. Do you want to see him?"

The king said: "Yes. Show him in."

He came before the king, and he said: "Your Royal Highness, I brought you a crown. A king's crown." Good. He removed the cloth and put the dish on the king's head. As the king was wearing it, the dish looked like a crown. It looked as though it was all diamonds, pearls, and precious stones. Everybody admired it; it was beautiful. They said they had not seen anything as beautiful in a long time, not as beautiful as this, as the vessel the poor Jew had brought.

The king said to them: "Look here, give this man whatever he wants."

They said to him: "This man is homeless, and he has many children."

The king said: "Give him a good house to live in. Furnish it, give him household goods—bedsteads, mattresses, whatever he wants. And tell him to come here every month and collect his salary, the salary of a king's deputy."

The poor Jew returned home a rich man, very, very rich.

It was the Eve of Pessah. The rich man, his brother, had forgotten all about him. But now, on the Eve of Pessah he remembered. When they were all sitting at the festive tables celebrating Pessah and enjoying a lovely meal, the rich brother said to his wife: "Look here, I have just remembered my poor brother. I do not know if he

---

kind of earthenware pot shaped like a funnel without a neck and pierced with little holes in the bottom. The keskas is on the kedra, the edges of which are wrapped in cloth to prevent the steam from escaping between the two vessels.

is celebrating or if he is not, but let us send him a few Matzoth with some wine anyway."

His wife replied: "Good. I am not going to say 'No'—God forbid! After all, he is your brother."

The rich brother called his servant-girl. He gave her a packet of Matzoth and a couple of bottles of wine, and he told her to go to his brother's house. She went to where the brother had been living before. There was nobody there. She asked the neighbors: "The man that used to live here—where is he?"

They said to her: "What do you want him for? He is a rich man, he returned a very rich man, as rich as the king."

She kept looking and asking for him until finally she spotted the house. She walked up to the door. A servant-girl came and said to the rich man's servant-girl: "What is it you want?"

—"I was sent by the brother of the master of this house, he told me to bring . . ."

She replied: "Just put it here, and I will take you to my master, he will speak to you." The servant-girl took her to the brother. He said to her: "Oh yes, come here, take off those clothes, and put on new ones, new, beautiful clothes, and be properly dressed. Would you like to join us for the rest of the Seder?"

She said to him: "I must go back; he is waiting; I must not keep him waiting. I will go and tell him everything." Good. She returned to her master and said: "You put me to shame. I am returning the things you told me to bring to your brother. You put me to shame. You see, neither your house nor anyone else's and not even the king's house contains what your brother's house contains."

—"What is that you are saying?"

She said: "You heard me. It's exactly the way I told you."

He would not believe her. He sent another servant. The servant came back and said: "Look at the clothes I wore when I went there. I took them off when I came to that place, and they threw them on the garbage heap."

Still he would not believe it, and he sent yet another servant. When she came back, she told him the same thing. So what did he do? He spoke to his wife, and he said to her: "Look here, let's not have a Seder tonight. Let's just pay my brother a visit and see what's going on there, where he got all this [money] from."

He went to see his brother. The brother was very friendly; he was glad to see him, he and his children and everybody. They offered him a seat. When he saw that, he said: "Now my eldest son must marry your eldest daughter."

They prepared a big wedding feast, and they were glad, but the rich brother still bore his brother a grudge, and he wanted to know where he got all this great wealth from. He spoke to him, saying: "Explain. Just tell me."

He replied: "Remember, this baby is now two months old. Before he was born, I went to see you and I told you I did not have anything to keep him warm and I did not have any food for my wife, and she was in a bad way. But you did not give me anything, and on my way back home I was in tears. Then I met someone who gave me a piece of advice, telling me what to do. So I rushed to the market and bought some earthenware vessel to make kuskus in, and I took it to the king, and the king gave me all this."

The Pessah holiday was over. The rich brother went to the market and bought lots of those kuskus dishes, loaded them onto a donkey and took them to the king's palace. When he came to the door, they said to him: "What is this?"

He said to them: "I have heard that the king likes these dishes."
—"Fine. Who told you so?"
He replied: "I heard it."

Good. The guards went to the king and told him about the man. The king said: "Do not show him in. Just make him stand at the entrance, so everybody can grab one of those dishes and hit him till his body is smashed to smithereens."

That was his punishment.

## Commentary: IFA 16604

### THE MIRACLE THAT OCCURRED
### BETWEEN PURIM AND PESSAH

Typologically, this narrative belongs to International Type Aarne-Thompson 1689 A: "Two presents to the king." However, this narrative, as well as other Jewish parallel narratives undergo oicotypification, reflecting values, norms, and Jewish customs and the real-life situations of the narrating society.

The IFA have twenty-three versions of this narrative type; two of them use the motif of a pot or dish serving as a crown, in parallel with this narrative.[1]

---

[1] The narratives are from various ethnic groups: Morocco (4), Egypt (2), Sefardi Israel (3), Ashkenazi Israel (1), Samaritans (1), Karaites (1), Yemen (1), Iraqi Kurdistan (6), Iraq (6), Persia (1), Romania (1), Poland (1). For a version in print, see Stahl 1976, no. 11.

A cup and a plate for Kiddush and Havdala (ceremonies at beginning and conclusion of Sabbath and holidays), twentieth century. By kind permission of the Israel Museum, Jerusalem.

The narrative is constructed on the concept of foolish imitation, which was exhaustively treated by Luethi (Luethi 1980, 3–12). The narrative consists of two central episodes linked by connecting episodes. The central episodes are structurally symmetric: in each the protagonist comes to the king's palace and gives the king a present. As distinct from the structural symmetry there is, however, a difference in contents: the poor man acts upon divine guidance and has no evil motives, and he is therefore rewarded. But the rich man is motivated by greed and is consequently punished—Motif J 2401: "Foolish imitation results in death."

The confrontation is against an economic background, but it gains momentum when a confrontation that has another background is added. The rich man disregards not only the social value of helping the poor but also the most sacred Jewish social value— mutual assistance within the family.

105

The narrative is located in the most critical period of the Jewish year, the time between Purim and Pessah, the time to prepare for the Seder. It involves much preparation and is moreover costly. That the rich man failed to ask his poor brother to spend the night of the Seder at his house, although he knew that he was penniless, and that he only remembered him on the night of the Seder makes him a negative character who fails to observe the commandments of man's relation to man and man's relation to his God. His actions as well as his greed, represented by his foolish imitation, cause the audience to loathe him and to gloat over his punishment at the end of the narrative.

Many narratives constructed on the principle of foolish imitation are realistic and belong to the genre of the novella of cleverness or foolishness, respectively. This narrative is a sacred legend. The protagonist is not clever: the decision to bring the king a kuskus dish is not his own. He is guided by divine providence: the gates of Heaven open, and a messenger comes and advises the man what to do. When he places the crown on the king's head "it was as though studded with jewels and pearls and precious stones" signifying divine intervention. In this respect it is very much like the Jewish oicotype Aarne-Thompson *750 (IFA): "The two washer women."[2]

It is also similar to this oicotype because of the time of year in which the narrative is set—that is, before the Pessah holiday with its central values and norms that include the unity and coherence of the family seated at the Seder table. Moreover, both narratives deal with foolish imitation, and both belong to the genre of the sacred legend; the only difference is that the characters in our narrative are men, whereas the characters in oicotype Aarne-Thompson *750 (IFA) are women.

In addition to values and norms, the narrative reflects the customs of the narrating society that include marriage between cousins and the eating of kuskus, the Moroccan staple food. In addition it is interesting to observe the realities of life in modern Israel which the narrator includes in his traditional narrative. When the narrator tells the audience in what dire straits the poor man was, he hastens to add "in those days the government did not help . . .". Undoubtedly, this remark contrasts conditions in Morocco with the new realities of life in Israel.

---

[2] For an exhaustive treatment of this oicotype, see Shenhar and Bar-Itzhak 1981, 160–164.

# *The Birth of the Maharal*[1]

FROM: RABBI ḤANANIA PORTAL

This story happened long ago, just before the Maharal was born. It happened on the eve of Pessah. The Maharal's mother was in labor. In those days the Jews would be charged with the murder of a Christian whose blood they allegedly used to prepare the Matzah of Pessah. This is what they would do to the Jews before every holiday.

Now it happened that a Christian who hated Jews wanted to bring false charges against the Jews. He removed the body of a Christian from the churchyard. The body of a man who had died shortly before Pessah. He carried the body from the churchyard in a sack and dropped it at the rabbi's house, Rabbi Bezalel, the Maharal's father, saying: "They are going to find it, and they are going to say 'There! The rabbi has killed the Christian because he wants his blood for the Matzoth.'"

That very night the rabbi's wife went into labor, and there was a great commotion in the house. Several people came to help. The midwife lived far away, and they wanted to go and bring her to the rabbi's house. They rushed out to fetch her. The Christian, who was an enemy of the Jews, saw them run, and he too started running so they should not catch him. They run—he runs, they run—he runs, they run—he runs.

The watchmen saw a man running and other men running in pursuit of him. They said: "Surely this man has stolen something, and they are trying to catch him." The watchmen caught him, opened the sack, and found the corpse. They said: "What is this?"

They took the Christian to the police station and kept him there till morning. In the meanwhile, the people who were running to fetch the midwife found her and brought her to the rabbi's house, and this is how the Maharal was born. That is when you say, "There was a miracle."

In the morning they questioned the man, and the man pleaded guilty, saying he had taken the corpse in order to drop it at the rabbi's house so people should say the rabbi had killed a Christian for his blood because he needed it for the Matzoth.

---

[1] Rabbi Yehuda Liva Ben-Betzalel; see commentary.

An amulet for guarding the baby and mother after birth, probably nineteenth century. Y. Aynhorn collection. By kind permission of the Israel Museum, Jerusalem.

The rabbi knew nothing about it, and the people who had brought the midwife did not know anything about it either. On the following day, which was Pessah, the governor sent for the rabbi. A messenger came to the rabbi's house and said: "The governor wants you." The rabbi replied: "You know today is a Jewish holiday, don't you? I cannot go to the governor's house on a holiday. Perhaps I can come tomorrow?" But he said: "No. You have to go right now."

The rabbi went to the governor's house.

The governor said to him: "What did they steal yesterday? Was anything stolen from your house?"—"No, God forbid."

The governor continued: "Then why were there so many people at your house, and why did they all rush out?"

He answered: "They rushed out to bring the midwife because my wife was in labor."

And the rabbi explained all of it to the governor.

The governor said to the rabbi: "I want you to know that a miracle happened to you. I will issue an ordinance prohibiting blood libel as of today."

## *Commentary:* IFA 16605

### THE BIRTH OF THE MAHARAL

The narrative belongs to Jewish oicotype Aarne-Thompson *730E (IFA): "He who keeps Israel will neither sleep nor slumber," which has thirteen parallels in IFA.[1] Two central elements combine in the narrative: On the one hand, a saint's legend deals with the special circumstances of the birth of the Maharal, whereas on the other hand, a sacred legend about the Pessah holiday deals with a blood libel[2] and the reversal of the false charges brought against the Jews. In the Diaspora, blood libel at Pessah was one of the most serious charges the Jews had to face.

The Maharal, Rabbi Yehuda Liva Ben-Betzalel, is a saintly figure in Jewish folklore. He was born in Poznan, Poland, in 1520 and died in Prague in 1609. He was a rabbi in Nicolsburg, Moravia, until 1598 when he became the Rabbi of Prague. The most famous legend about the Maharal is about the creation of the Golem.[3]

When a number of saint's legends were investigated, the percentage of narratives centering on the birth of the saint proved small as compared with those focusing on the mature saint or the saint after his death (Noy 1967, 106–133; Bar-Itzhak 1987, 190–195). Yet in the majority of cases there was at least one legend about the saint's birth. The circumstances of the saint's birth are invariably exceptional, and hence they add an aura of sanctity that links up with the metaphysical dimension of the saint. Many folktales about the birth of holy characters follow the pattern of the birth of a mythic hero (Raglan 1936; Rank 1959).[4]

In our narrative the birth of the Maharal occurs in prime time of the Jewish year, that is, on the eve of the Pessah holiday. The timing of the birth suggests that the character is holy. But in the narrative the birth also connects with the deliverance of his people: the libelous charges were dropped.

The archetypal element attached to the Pessah holiday—deliverance of the Jewish people from slavery in Egypt—recurs here

---

[1] The parallel narratives are found in Morocco (2), Sefardi Israel (2), Ashkenazi Israel (1), Yemen (1), Persian Kurdistan (1), Iraq (2), Georgia (1), Caucasus (1), Poland (2).

[2] For an exhaustive treatment of "blood libel," see Noy 1967; Dundes 1991.

[3] The IFA has twelve narratives about the Maharal.

[4] For a discussion of the subject, see Bar-Itzhak, ibid., 144–146.

in the context that is relevant to the narrating society: the Jewish people are acquitted of the charges of blood libel leveled against them; this is the most dangerous charge leveled against Jews in the Diaspora. Thus, an implied parallel is established between Moses, who saved his people in ancient times, and the Maharal, who saved his people in the story. This, of course, contributes to the glorification of the Maharal.

In blood libel narratives holy supernatural characters may sometimes intervene actively. In the majority of cases the Prophet Elijah saves the Jews. In our narrative God Almighty and His messengers do not take any active part, but the narrative implies divine intervention inasmuch as the Maharal's mother goes into labor precisely at the critical moment, just in time to stop the impending disaster.

# Rabbi Ḥaim Ben Atar[1]

FROM: RABBI ḤANANIA PORTAL

Rabbi Ḥaim Ben Atar was a poor man. To make a living, he worked at a trade: he was a skilled tailor.

In those days, people used to sew what is called a *kaftan* in Arabic. A kaftan is a flowing robe worn by the children of kings. None but the children of kings wore a kaftan. The children of kings. And Rabbi Ḥaim Ben Atar knew how to weave kaftans and how to sew them.

The daughter of the king who reigned in those days was getting married, and the king needed to give her dresses that were to be her dowry. The king sent for the tailor-in-chief and commanded him to get the dresses sewn. Now the only person able to sew the kind of dresses the king wanted was the rabbi, Rabbi Ḥaim Ben Atar.

Rabbi Ḥaim Ben-Atar followed a certain routine. One or two days a week he would sew a couple of clothes and then collect his pay. Thereafter he would not go out anymore; he would just sit in the Yeshiva and teach the students. He would only go out again when he had no more money left. Then he would go out again and work at his trade. The week the king's daughter wanted to get married, he

---

[1] See commentary.

had money. The tailor-in-chief came and said to the rabbi: "Take this! The king wants to make the wedding feast for his daughter, and I want you to do the sewing."

The rabbi replied: "I cannot go out before next week."

—"What is that you are saying?"

—"You heard me."

The clothes did not get sewn, the day of the wedding was approaching, and the king sent for the tailor-in-chief: "Where are the clothes?"

He replied: "What am I to do? The rabbi who knows how to sew the clothes you want refuses to work."

The king sent for Rabbi Ḥaim Ben Atar and said: "Why didn't you sew the clothes?"

—"I never do any sewing before I run out of money. That is my way of doing things. As long as I have money, I do not work. I study the Tora. When I run out of money, I start working. Right now I have enough money to last me till the coming week, thank God."

The king said: "How can you do this to the king?" He had him arrested.

When someone was sentenced to death, they would throw him into a pit full of lions, tigers, and other wild beasts. Rabbi Ḥaim Ben Atar was tried and sentenced to the pit. Good. He said to them: "Look here, I am going to take some of my books; you do whatever you want."

He took a sack and the books he needed into it: Jewish law, as well as Tsitsith[2] and Tefillin,[3] and all he needed. He said to them: "First you throw the sack into the pit, and next you throw me down there."

They threw down the sack filled with books, and then they threw him down. And they knew it: when a person who had been sentenced to death was left in the pit for the night, they would find nothing but the bones the next day. In the morning, they came to collect the bones and bury them. Now the rabbi, Rabbi Ḥaim Ben Atar, may God rest his soul, had gone down into the pit, had taken out his books, wrapped himself in the Tallith, and put on the Tefillin. And all the wild beasts surrounded him, just like his students. And he studies, and they do not do him any harm. In the morning all the king's watchmen come to see what happened and to collect the bones. They found Rabbi Ḥaim Ben Atar standing there, praying,

---

[2] A fringed garment worn by observant Jews.

[3] Phylacteries.

reading aloud, with all the beasts listening to him. They went to the king's palace and told him. He said to them: "I do not believe you."

—"If you don't believe us, come and see for yourself."

The king found the rabbi standing inside the pit, studying the Tora. The rabbi carries no arms, and the lions and the tigers and all the beasts listen to him; they listen to what he is reading to them. The king said: "This man is a saint. We must not say anything to him."

He told his men to pull the rabbi up, out of the pit. The rabbi said to them: "Do not pull me up before you get my things, the books and the Tallith. First you pull up my books, and then you get me out." And that is what they did.

This is the story of the miracle that occurred to Rabbi Ḥaim Ben Atar.

## Commentary: IFA 16606

### RABBI ḤAIM BEN ATAR

The narrative belongs to oicotype Aarne-Thompson *776 (IFA): "Miscellaneous Divine Rewards."[1] The genre is the saint's legend—a "Shevah," in Jewish terminology, about one of the most admired and sacred rabbis of Moroccan Jews, Rabbi Ḥaim Ben Atar. Rabbi Ḥaim Ben Atar was born in Sali, Morocco, in 1696 and died in Jerusalem in 1743. He lived for few years in Livorno, and his famous book *Or ha'ḥaim* was printed there in 1739 and became very popular among the Hasidim in Europe. He arrived to Jerusalem in 1742 and established there a Yeshiva that after his death was called Yeshivat Or ha'Ḥaim.

The most important feature of the saint's legend is the centrality of a character whom the narrating society regards as holy.

---

[1] Of this oicotype 106 versions are registered in IFA. They were narrated by members of the following ethnic groups: Morocco (27), Algeria (1), Tunisia (13), Libya (1), Egypt (9), Greece (3), Syria (4), Ashkenazi Israel (6), Sefardi Israel (12), Arab Israel (2), Yemen (14), Iraqi Kurdistan (3), Persian Kurdistan (1), Turkish Kurdistan (1), Iraq (16), Persia (11), Bukhara (6), Afghanistan (4), India (3), Georgia (2), Caucasus (2), Rumania (2), Poland (14), Latvia (3), Russia (6).

The following were published: Aminof 1974, nos. 3, 4, 12—Bukhara; Attias 1976, no. 17—Greece; Baharav 1968, no. 29—Persia; no. 37—Iraqi Kurdistan; Cheichel 1970 no. 11—Bukhara, no. 14—Morocco; Cheichel 1973, no. 11—Poland; Haviv 1966, no. 5—Morocco; Mizrahi 1967, no. 29—Persia; Noy 1963b, no. 47—Yemen; Noy 1966 no. 69—Tunisia; Noy 1979, no. 13—Tunisia.

A mantle for a Tora Scroll. Mapa De'sifer. 1864. Y. Aynhorn collection. By kind permission of the Israel Museum, Jerusalem.

This character is an object of veneration to be emulated and identified with. Noy proposed the classification of these legends according to the period of time in the saint's life (Noy 1967, 106–133). An investigation of narratives about three Jewish saints proves that the majority of legends focus on the mature period in the protagonist's life (Noy 1967; Bar-Itzhak 1987, 190–195) when he is at his best, well known and held in high esteem. This applies to our narrative, too. The value our narrative wishes to establish as holy is the study of the Tora, for this is the value the holy character in the narrative holds to be of paramount importance. Rabbi Ben Atar employs his time in two things: working at a trade and studying the Tora. Working at a trade is necessary only to keep the body alive, and therefore Rabbi Ben Atar refuses to work at his trade as long as he has enough money to sustain him. By contrast, studying the Tora is the goal that makes one's life meaningful.

On the plot level this worldview is expressed through the confrontation between the rabbi and the king. This confrontation classes the narrative with the tales about Judeo-gentile interaction. The rabbi is not prepared to forego the study of the Tora, whereas the king wants him to work at his trade and will not be disobeyed.

113

All saint's legends contain elements of the miraculous that suggest divine intervention in the lives of men. Man's good deeds are rewarded, and transgressions entail punishment. The miraculous element in our narrative is survival: having disobeyed the king, the rabbi is thrown into a pit full of predators, but his life is miraculously spared. Survival in a pit full of predators is a common motif in the Jewish folk narrative; moreover, it reminds us of ancient texts such as Daniel in the lions' den. That the Rabbi takes his books and the ritual objects used in prayer into the pit implies his determination to observe the commandments as well as his trust in God who will save his life. The miracle in the narrative serves a twofold purpose: it demonstrates the holiness of the rabbi, and it settles the confrontation between the Jews and the gentiles. The Jews are victorious, which reflects the wish of the narrating society that even the kings of the gentiles recognize the sanctity of Jewish rabbis.

The motif of the saint who tames ferocious wild beasts that surrender themselves to him also occurs in Christian folktales (Motifs B 251.211 and B 256). It has been exhaustively treated by Loomis (Loomis 1948, 63). In many Jewish versions the motif is linked to observance of the Sabbath. A Jew joins a convoy, and when the Sabbath comes he asks the wagoners to stop and wait till after the Sabbath. The wagoners refuse to do so, and although he is left behind and all by himself he makes all the necessary preparations for the Sabbath. This is described in IFA 8136: "As the rabbi prays he notices a lion in the distance which is approaching. The rabbi did not interrupt his prayer and his songs, and as soon as the lion approaches the area around the rabbi, it kneels and lies down and does not cross the line. The rabbi says all his prayers, blesses the wine, eats his meal, recites another blessing and goes to sleep. The lion watches over him, and when the Sabbath ends it carries him to the convoy."[2]

The motif of Sabbath observance is absent from our narrative that highlights the value of Tora study. But in both narratives the fact that the rabbi is saved from the wild animals causes the gentiles to recognize the holiness of the character. And as in our narrative, so in IFA 8136, the gentiles accept his holiness and submit themselves to him: "Whenever the rabbi said 'let us wait,' the guides would stop and wait. . . ."

---

[2] Cheichel 1970, no. 11.—Bukhara.

# YAMNA DAYAN

**WHEN WE** recorded the folktales, Yamna Dayan was about seventy years old. She came from Kal'ah in the district of Marakesh. Her father's name was Mass'ud and her mother's name was Zohara.

When Yamna was six, she contracted an eye disease. The doctors who tried to cure her in fact caused her condition to worsen, and she became totally blind. Although she could no longer see, she learned how to sew and embroider the traditional dress, Farajee'ah. Her work was so beautiful that people said she was a better craftswoman than many of those who could see.

She came to Israel in 1955. In Shlomi, she lived with her nephew and his wife, who were taking good care of her and an ailing mother.

Yamna had no formal education, but she learned a great deal from the folk narratives told by her family, the local rabbi, and friends in the old country. When we recorded her, she said she still had an opportunity to listen to folk narratives on weekdays and holidays and on special occasions such as a Brith-Milah, a wedding, or when mourners offered their condolences to a bereaved family. She herself would offer folk narratives when she had visitors or when she met other women on special occasions, on holidays, and when visiting the sick.

# What is Written in Heaven Cannot be Wiped Out

FROM: YAMNA DAYAN

There was a Ḥakham (Rabbi) who would sit in the Yeshiva day in and day out. He had forty students whom he taught. His wife did not bear children; she was barren, the poor woman.

One of God's fine days the wife is sitting in her house, and lo and behold! two Jewish women come.

They said to her: "Where, oh my sister, is the Ḥakham?"

She said to them: "Oh my daughters, the Ḥakham is in the Yeshiva all day long. I send his midday meal there, and he does not return before nightfall. Each evening he returns. What do you want him for?"

They said to her: "Oh my daughter, we do not bear children, and we were told that with his help women conceive. We, too, want from him and from God that he should write an amulet for us and we bear a child, be it a boy or a girl."

She said to them: "If the physician could cure, he would cure himself. I, too, do not bear children, and why did he not write any Kame'a[1] for me?"

They said to her: "Oh my daughter, that is what people told us."

She said to them: "Come to him in the evening. He is not here during the day."

These Jewesses departed.

The wife got up and made her bed and went to sleep.

The husband returns in the evening, the Ḥakham returns, and finds his wife, who would always prepare the evening meal and boil the kettle to make tea, and here she is—asleep.

—"What is the matter with you, why were you sleeping?"

---

[1] Amulet in Hebrew.

She said to him: "Sick."

He said to her: "How? You were well when I left."

She said to him: "Why do you write amulets for Jewesses so they should bear children, and for us, who do not even have a mewing cat in the house, you do not write any?

He said to her: "Oh my daughter, I wait for God to bring me children. But if you want me to write you an amulet, I will make a dream question, and what they answer me I will tell you."

The next morning my dear friend[2] rose, pared his fingernails, and immersed himself in the Mikveh,[3] and she did so too: she dressed, putting on new clothes, all clean, she went to the ritual bath and returned.

They slept.

During the night, the Maggid[4] appeared to him and said to him: "Do you want a daughter? She will be forced to convert on her wedding night. Do you want a son—he will not have any luck." He awoke, and said to his wife: "What?"

She said to him: "This is what I dreamt."

He said to her: "I too dreamt the same dream; this is what they told me."

She said to him: "And what are we going to do?"

He said to her: "Will I not feel ashamed? I am a great Ḥakham, a man who teaches others, and they will hear that my daughter was forced to convert on her wedding night?! Let's ask him for a son, at least we will keep the commandments—the commandment of circumcision and the commandment of the redemption of the firstborn. As long as we are alive, we will give him food and drink, and raise him, and when we die—God will provide for him."

They talked it over. When the Maggid came to them, he said: "What have you decided?"

He told him: "Give us a son."

She got up at night.[5]

Good. Don't you say anything except this:[6] the woman conceived, three months in heat, three months getting fat—three—she

---

[2] A term of endearment used by the narrator when referring to the Ḥakham.

[3] A ritual bath.

[4] A messenger sent by God, literrally "sayer" or "teller." For an exhaustive treatment, see Patai 1990, 202–220. The narrator uses an ancient Hebrew word, although she narrates the folktale in Judeo-Arabic.

[5] The narrator implies that they had sexual intercourse; modesty prevents her from being explicit.

[6] A typical connector.

clutched the rope. "He who saves from trouble, may He save her from trouble."

She had a son. The townspeople did not know what to do, so overjoyed were they, "The Ḥakham of our town has a son! The Ḥakham of our town has a son!"

They come, they bring presents, they bring gifts, good. For seven days they rejoiced; the child was circumcised; the ceremony of redemption of the firstborn was performed.

People grow as we count the years, and he grew "between the table and the tablecloth";[7] he kept on growing in the daytime and at night. The child grew up; his father took him to the Yeshiva and taught him. The parents give him food and drink, as much as he wants; they loved him so.

Good, they are alive, and God provides for them, and he studies, studies, studies.

Before she gave birth, the wife [was told that her] brother-in-law was in dire straits. Her husband was a Ḥakham and wealthy, and his brother—he needed God's help, he had nothing.

On the eve of Passover, the Ḥakham's wife came and said to her husband: "We are going to send them something, but that is not enough. Your brother has children, bring them so they can spend all of the Passover holidays with us. When the holidays are over, they will go back to their house, and God will help them and provide for them."

He said to her: "If that is your will, it is my will too."

She sent someone to invite his niece.

She came.

The Ḥakham said to her: "Help my wife with the preparations for the Passover, with the kosher-for-Passover and the not-kosher-for-Passover, and stay with her."

She said to him: "Very well, oh my uncle."

Good, she helped her with all the household chores. Whatever her aunt was doing, she helped her. Until the eve of Passover.

She sent her away and told her: "Go and bring your mother and your brothers. Bring them all, so they can celebrate together with us."

Good, they celebrated, they ate and drank, and the girl blesses the house, wishing them there should always be plenty of food.

She said to her: "Oh my uncle's wife who has made us happy

---

[7] Here dough was left to rise. The narrator uses the image in order to highlight the speed at which the child was growing.

and has brought us here for the Passover holiday and did not leave us sad—may God make her happy."

(As God listened to her wish, so may He listen to you and listen to me and bless Yaacob ben Zohara).[8]

The woman bore the child, and the girl took care of him. He was three months old, four months.

The mother heard that a certain Ḥakham had died.

She said to the girl: "Oh my daughter, I leave the child in your care. Watch over him, and I will go to the Ḥakham's house and show my face and come back."

Good. She nursed the child, fed him, and put him to sleep next to the girl, in a push-cart or a cradle, and left. And the daughter of her brother-in-law stayed with him. She took a pillow and fell asleep alongside the child. The Maggid came; he stood over her in a dream and said to her: "Watch over this child, he is your 'Mazzal.'"[9]

She said: "Oh God! I am old enough to be a mother of three or four children. And now, do I have to wait for this baby to grow up and have his Bar-Mitzvah, and afterward I will marry him?!"

She slept. The Maggid came, he said to her: "I told you, do not hesitate, this is your 'luck.' Even if you climb to the sky—this is your lot. And when you climb down again—this is your lot."

She got up and started thinking.

She dressed the child, putting on his amulets and his clothes, and put him in a big box. The sea was in front of the house, and she threw him into the sea and went back to sleep.

His mother returned, looks in the pram—the child is not there. Right next to the girl—the child is not there. Where is he?

She woke the girl: "Where is the child?"

She told her: "I do not know. I left him right next to me, and I fell asleep. I woke, and as you see—he is not here."

The poor woman mourned and cried, and she did not leave anything undone.

The Ḥakham returned from the Yeshiva and put on sackcloth and fastened it with ropes. They had never had a child before, and now that they had the privilege of having one—such a calamity?!

They rose to weep and mourn. The poor girl—they did not let her go. They said: "Sit here with us and help us, and cook for us."

---

[8] The narrator asks for a blessing. Yaacob ben Zohara is her nephew, in whose house she is living.

[9] He is your "luck," your "intended," your future husband. In Hebrew the meaning of *Mazzal* is both luck and destiny.

119

She stayed in their house.

Now, mind you, let's move to the Ḥakham in another town. This Ḥakham cannot possibly be left without any fish on Friday.

The fishermen came and said to him: "Alas! We did not find any fish, Ḥakham, we found no fish in the sea. We throw the net, and it comes up empty."

He told them: "Just bring me a little piece, even if it is as small as a cup."

They went out to sea again, and threw the net, and there was a very large fish that had swallowed the box with the baby, and it got caught in the net. The fisherman tried to pull the fish up together with the net, but the fish was heavy. So he set the fish free and returned the net to the sea.

The Ḥakham said to him: "Bring me a piece of it, even if it is no bigger than the palm of a hand."

The poor fellows left and tried very hard; they tried with all their might and tried again until finally they pulled it up. They brought him the fish, and they dragged it as you drag a cow, and they placed the fish next to him.

Said the Ḥakham to his wife: "Go and clean the fish."

She told him that presently her daughter would go and do it: "Go and prepare the fish for us. At least cut off a piece and prepare that, and bring it to me so I can cook it before the Sabbath begins."

The girl went and started opening the fish with a pocket knife, and there! the baby was crying. She fled; she panicked. She dropped the knife and panicked.

She said to him: "Father."

He said to her: "Yes."

She said to him: "There is a human being inside the fish."

He said to her: "Who told you so?"

She said to him: "I made a cut with the knife, heard a baby cry."

He said to his wife: "You go. You know how to do it, and you leave her be. She is just a little girl, and she does not know how to do it."

The wife went off and worked carefully, till she had opened the fish and pulled out the box and opened it. In the box she found a perfect baby, well formed, the goats would not graze if they saw him.[10]

She said to him: "There is a human being inside the fish, here he is."

Good, she washed him and clothed him and put him [in a

---

[10] An image used to highlight the child's great beauty.

room] together with her children. She gave him the food and drink that is meant for babies: bananas, apples, and so on, until the child grew up. He would go to school together with her children, and he thought they were his brothers, his father and mother, and he did not know any other people.

Time passed. The child eats, drinks—just the same as their children—they leave together and return home together and eat and drink. Good. He grew and was a youth.

The children fought and quarreled in the synagogue, and as they were quarreling they said to him: "Do you think you are our brother? You are not our brother; we just found you inside a fish."

The child returned, cried, and would not eat and would not drink.

The father rose and said to him: "Oh my son, what happened to you? To be so sad—that is not your way. Usually you laugh with your brothers, eat and drink, and why do you not want to talk now?"

He said: "I am not their brother. Tell me who are my father and mother, tell me!"

He said: "Oh my son, if we did not beget you, how did you get here?"

He said: "Your children told me that you found me inside a fish."

He said: "Oh my son, Shema Israel, Adonay Eloheynu."[11]

He told him all that had happened.

—"And now, if you wish to stay here with us, as my children are so will you be. I will find you a wife and do everything for you."

He refused.

He told him: "I am going to ask you a favor. Wait until I buy you a Tallith and Tefillin and you pray everyday,[12] and then go away and look for your parents. Maybe God will lead you to them—here is the amulet that you wore around your neck. Look! your father's and mother's names are written on it."

He said: "Alright."

Good. He stayed with him, girded himself with the patience of an enemy. The Ḥakham made him a Bar-Mitzvah together with his

---

[11] Hear oh Israel, our Lord God. The whole biblical verse is "Shema Israel Adonay Eloheynu Adonay Eḥad" (Deuteronomy 6,6). Also cited in everyday prayer as the basic expression of faith. It became a verse cited by martyrs before their death. Among Moroccan Jews when a person retracts a false statement, he says "Hear Oh Israel!"

[12] I.e., after he has his Bar-Mitzvah.

own children, gave him food and drink and bought him Tefillin, a Tallith and books, everything that is necessary, and sent him away.

He said to him: "Go, oh my son. May God grant you only what is good, and may He help you find your parents."

He moved from one town to another, and the dear Almighty led him right to the doorstep, to his father's house.

And the house is full of rubbish, broken bottles, and glasses. Whenever somebody broke something, he would throw it there. There was no landlord to clear out the rubbish and clean the place.

He said: "I'll have a look at this place; perhaps this is where I will be redeemed."

As he was standing there, that very self-same girl approached, carrying rubbish she wanted to throw out.

She said to him: "Oh my brother, what do you want to do in this house?"

He said to her: "Why, who owns this place?"

She told him: "The owner is not here." (May this not happen to you!)[13]

He said to her: "Why is that?"

She said to him: "A certain Ḥakham, that is what happened to him."

She told him about the child . . .

He said to her: "Perhaps you would like to sweep the floor to make room for a mat for me to sit on, or a cushion to sit on. Anyway there is nobody around. I will get my books and sit down and read."

She entered, said to her uncle: "Uncle."

He said to her: "Yes."

She told him: "A youth who just started laying Tefillin—this is what he wants. He told me—just give me a cushion to sit on."

He told her: "Go, my child—if he would like to live with us, he is welcome. We are people who study, and there is an Almighty God. You bring him here, and whatever we live on he, too, will live on."

She said to him: "Alright."

She went off.

He said to her: "Enter this room, which has been locked for many years, and open it. Perhaps you will find a rug or something else to spread there."

She entered the room, opened it, took a rug or a mattress, swept a corner for him and made up a bed for him, and he sat down.

---

[13] The narrator's aside.

She made him a cup of tea or a cup of coffee so he should stay awake, and he sat down and read a book.

He said to the Ḥakham: "How is it, oh Ḥakham, that you mourn thus? If this child departed, there will be another."

He said: "We were childless until God took pity on us and gave us this child."

He remained with them for the Sabbath.

He said to the Ḥakham: "How did this happen, and how did this happen to the child?"

He told him: "Oh God, we left him with this girl, and we went to the house of a Ḥakham. When we returned, we did not find him.

"'Oh my daughter, where is the child?' She said: 'I did not see him. I fell asleep, I slept, and I did not see where he went and who took him away.'"

The girl said: "And now I will tell you what happened, uncle. This is what happened to me: I was told that he is "my luck," and here I was—grown up and single. Would I have to wait for this child to grow up? I became angry and said: 'This is what I will do to him.' I put him in a box and threw him into the sea."

"Oh my daughter, if only you had told me, I would have married you to him the same day, even though he was a little child, and I would gladly have raised him . . ."

She said to him: "This is what God gave and what my good sense told me to do."

Then the youth produced his amulet, and they found his father's and his mother's name and his own name inscribed on it.

The Ḥakham said: "God be praised, to-night, to-night, to-night, to-night I will marry you, I will marry you."

Good. The poor man rose, took off his mourning clothes, bathed himself and put on clean clothes—he and his wife. And there was no end to their happiness. The next day they called porters who cleared out all the rubbish. They swept the house and called the painters to have the place whitewashed. He married her to him before the Sabbath. He made her his wife.

Will that which is written in Heaven be wiped out? It won't.

## *Commentary:* IFA 16441

### WHAT IS WRITTEN IN HEAVEN
### CANNOT BE WIPED OUT

The narrator heard this story from her brother, who used to tell it when the family met. She, too, tells this story when all the family meet in her home, and according to her testimony she has told it several times this year.

When the narrator was asked to classify the story in her mother tongue, she said "Ma'asseh," in Hebrew. There is no doubt that the genre classification used by folklore researchers indicates that we are dealing with a sacred legend. According to Jason's definition (Jason 1971, 67) the sacred legend is a tale "which deals with the central problems of the individual and society, in which the holy power of the official religion solves the problems, in favor of the stability of the existing social order." Our tale deals with two central problems in the cycle of life: birth and marriage. It serves to prove that man cannot escape God's decree and should not try to do so. Typologically the tale belongs to the "tales of destiny": Aarne-Thompson 934 A—"Predestined Death"[1] - or, to be more precise, Aarne-Thompson 934* H—"A childless couple must choose between the birth of a girl who will be unhappy, and the birth of a son who will be poor"[2] and Aarne-Thompson 930*E (IFA)—"A match made in heaven."

A distinctly theodicist note is embedded in the story.[3] This is owing to the fact that in a religious society it is inevitable that believers should begin to have second thoughts about their faith once they are confronted with certain cruel facts of life. It is therefore necessary to explain these facts, even though they appear cruel, to resolve the contradictions and the oddities in order to justify what has been decreed. In our story, for instance, the problem of sterility has to be explained: if the laws of reward and punishment work, then why should the wife of the just rabbi be infertile? Why should he have forty students and not even a single son? The answer is, of course, that infertility is not caused by the absence of divine provi-

---

[1] For tales of destiny, cf. Schwarzbaum 1968.

[2] Parallels from Tunisia, Turkey, Iraq, Persia, and India are recorded in IFA.

[3] The motif that none but God makes matches (T 53.4) occurs as early as the Talmudic-Midrashic tale of the matron and Rabbi Yossi ben Ḥalafta.

Parokhet, a curtain for the Holy Ark, probably twentieth century. Y. Aynhorn collection. By kind permission of the Israel Museum, Jerusalem.

dence or its perversion, but follows a hidden plan that is revealed only to those who know the secret and who can pierce the veil (i.e., the rabbi). God is not only to be judged by what is visible (i.e., on the level of the present time) because there is a secret connected to the future.[4] In our story, infertility averts a cruel fate: that is, conversion to Islam if the child to be born is a girl, and poverty if the child is a boy.

We know, of course, that if a child is born after many years of infertility, life has a special fate in store, as was already shown in the biblical stories about the Jewish ancestors. The absence of concrete details of "bad luck" in our narrative raises different expectations in the audience, who were raised on these stories. And surely, both the international religious view and the Jewish belief that man "cannot escape his fate" is illustrated and concretized as the action proceeds. Marriages, too, are decreed by the Almighty, and His decision cannot be reversed. Man can learn what God has decreed, and no more than that. The reasons why the girl wants to prevent her future marriage clearly emerge as the story unfolds. The difference

---

[4] Aarne-Thompson 930, cf. Shenhar 1974, no. 2 and note.

125

in age in this story is replaced by the "prophecy" in the international story of this type, and in the version of the Midrash Tanḥuma[5] it is substituted by difference in social class. The king's daughter wants to marry a poor man, and in this way social intermarriage bridges class difference. In the Jewish story religio-ethnic differences are sometimes added.

But this does not detract from the seriousness of the deed, for the girl is the rabbi's niece; that is, she is a relative, and hence what she does is judged more cruel than a stranger's treacherous behavior. She does not dare kill the baby but merely exposes him, and this enables her to say: "I did not shed his blood—his fate is in God's hands."

Incidentally, there is a symbolic-sexual parallel between the various versions of exposure (or concealment) of the future bridegroom or bride when mating is to be prevented: the bridegroom is thrown into a well or a pit or into the sea, and the bride is incarcerated in a tower, like King Solomon's daughter in the legend in Midrash Tanḥuma.

Our story is a women's story: it is narrated by a woman, and the main characters are women: after the visit of the two women, the rabbi's wife makes him act so their child should be born, and the niece takes matters in hand and exposes the baby. This is probably owing to the fact that infertility is thought to be a women's problem, and for this reason plot development is mainly connected to women.

Moreover, there seems to be a religious aura about the story. It presupposes a numinous and miraculous worldview. It opens with a rabbi who has "writing power," and it is suggested that by means of dream questions it is possible to commune with the worlds beyond, with the Maggid acting as the intermediary. Incidentally, the narrator says the word "Maggid" in Hebrew, using an ancient word, as distinct from certain modern Hebrew words that she sometimes uses in her stories. Somehow, the sanctity inherent in a word helps to delineate a character who is set aside as sacred.

The motif of the miraculous rescue of a human being by a fish that swallows him (F 911.4) ties in with the story of Jonah and the legend of Joshua Bin Nun, whose mother put him in a box and floated it down the sea, lest the prophecy be fulfilled that he would cut off his father's head. Joshua Bin Nun's life was saved because God appointed a fish to swallow him.[6]

---

[5] Buber 1885, preface, p. 136.

[6] Ginzberg 1966–1975, 5: 1; and note p. 119.

That the son is left on the doorstep of his father's house—"I'll have a look at this place, perhaps this is where I will be redeemed"—shows that God intervenes and participates in the course of events.

The pious atmosphere is also reflected in the studiousness of the rabbi, in the couple's observance of the rules of purification and ritual immersion, in the decision to have a son because this will permit them to observe commandments—that is, not only the commandment of "Be fruitful and multiply," but also of circumcision and redemption of the firstborn, of comforting mourners, and arranging a Bar-Mitzvah. That the child is rescued equally results from observance of a commandment, the commandment of honoring the Sabbath. The rabbi of another town would not usher in the Sabbath without some fish—a motif with which we are familiar from the story of Yoseph-Mokir-Shabbat (Shabbat, 119).

Thematically the story consists of four units, as follows:

1. The miraculous birth of a child.
2. The child is left in the care of his cousin, in fulfillment of the prophecy.
3. The child is miraculously rescued and grows up in another town.
4. He returns and marries his cousin, in fulfillment of the prophecy.

The first two units are laid in the same space, but the third relocates to a new space. Relocation is to be understood as man's attempt to escape his fate. His return to the earlier space symbolizes difficulties that have been overcome, and it is a prerequisite for the fulfillment of the prophecy. The story is an example of space as a symbol in the folk narrative.

It is interesting to note how the narrator rearranges the thematic units when she narrates the tale. The tale was recorded on two other occasions. In our version, the story begins with a childless rabbi, and the poverty-stricken brother whose daughter is adopted by the rabbi to take care of the baby is only introduced after the miraculous birth. But the two other recorded versions open with two brothers, one wealthy and the other poor. Both are typical openings of the folk narrative, and the narrator uses different improvisational approaches as she moves on to the central point, the complication—when the niece abandons the child. Because it is possible to get to this point by different routes, the narrator can afford to use different openings. It is, therefore, an example of the creativity of the folk narrator, who uses traditional units but shapes the manner of narration and improvisation according to her own needs, recreating the story over and over again whenever she narrates it in different performance situations.

The narrator Yamna Dayan, like the narrator Ḥaviva Dayan, embeds certain well known phrases in her tales. In her tale she uses the traditional saying used to describe pregnancy and birth: "Three months in heat, three months—getting fat, and three—she clutches the rope. He who saves from trouble, may he save her from trouble." The narrator need not recite the whole sentence because the audience is familiar with it. An interesting metaphor describes the speed at which the child grows. The image used is baking, a woman's work: "He grows [like dough that is left to rise] between the table and the table-cloth." Another interesting image is used to convey the beauty of the youth: "When the goats see him, they stop grazing."

A further point of interest is the link between the tale and the performance situation. When the narrator told us the story she was living in the home of her nephew. He and his wife have no children, and the tale was narrated in the presence of the wife, who takes good care of Yamna. It may be assumed that the opening, which deals with infertility followed by a miraculous birth, is not accidental and serves to answer the secret wishes of the people living in this house. However, the tale also affords the narrator an opportunity of expressing more overt wishes that cannot, however, be explicitly verbalized in conversation, because the subject is delicate. Hence the blessing, that is interwoven with the story, is the vehicle for expression. When the girl in the tale blesses her aunt, asking God to grant her happiness, the narrator at once extends the blessing to include her nephew: "As God granted her request (i.e., the girl's request), so may He grant your request and mine and bless Yaacob ben Zohara," that is, her nephew. The performance of this tale in this specific narrative situation is a reciprocal social act, and the story and the wishes and hopes expressed in it sublimate the wishes of the people living in the house in which it is narrated.[7]

---

[7] The use of the fable as a social reciprocal act is discussed by Kirshenblatt-Gimblett 1974, 106–130.

# *Queen Alfahima*

### From: Yamna Dayan

God was everywhere, and there was a certain king. His wife was called Alfahima because she understood many things.

One day two traders appeared with a pregnant she-ass and a pregnant mare. The she-ass gave birth, and the mare gave birth. The two of them gave birth. The owner of the she-ass stealthily placed the newborn ass with the mare, and the foal with the she-ass.

The next morning the owner of the mare started shouting. He said to the owner of the she-ass: "This is not the newborn foal."

The other man said: "That is what she brought forth. Finished." He came and had a look. They found the newborn ass suckling from the mare because she had started nursing the newborn ass with her eyes closed and had got used to him.

At this point, they went to the king for a decision. They were tried by the king.

He said to the king: "Sir, may God bless you. We brought these animals here while they were still pregnant, and they gave birth at night, and now the newborn ass is nursed by the mare, and the newborn foal is being nursed by the she-ass."

The king said to them: "Good, match them, and we shall see. If he suckles, the young ass was born to the mare, and if he doesn't, he is not her foal."

Good, they brought the animals, and the young ass suckled from the mare.

The owner of the mare, the poor man, he started crying bitterly, and his cries rise to the sky, and he says: "No mare will ever give birth to an ass."

And he leaves, crying all the time.

As he was crying and screaming, the owner of the mare said to the owner of the she-ass: "A foal born to a mare cannot be a young ass."

When the king's wife heard how they were arguing, she said to them: "What is the matter with you, you two guys? Why are you fighting?"

They said: "May God bless you. Last night we brought the

mare and the she-ass, and both were pregnant. During the night, they gave birth."

The owner of the mare addressed the king's wife, saying: "This man says that the mare gave birth to an ass, and the she-ass gave birth to a foal."

She said to him: "Listen! Go and get a fish. Let it be a big fish, and get a stick and hit the fish. Keep on beating the fish right in front of the king, till he says: 'Oh, oh, what do you want with this fish? What are you beating it for?' Then you tell him: 'This fish ate my field of cucumbers.' When he tells you: 'Can there be such a thing as a fish eating cucumbers?' you tell him: 'Can there be such a thing as a mare giving birth to an ass?'"

They left, as has been related, they left. He stood next to the king, and he started beating the fish with the stick, beating it again and again.

Then the king spoke to him. He said: "What do you want with this fish, you wicked man? What are you beating this fish for?"

He said to him: "Sir, may God bless you. The fish ate my field of cucumbers."

The king said to him: "Can there ever be such a thing as a fish eating cucumbers?"

And the man said: "Can there ever be such a thing as a mare giving birth to an ass?"

The king said: "Oh dear me, it is my wife Alfahima, she is the one who told you to do this."

He kept silent.

Then he went back and took the ass. He returned the newborn ass to its mother, and he returned the newborn foal to its mother. The king left, and they left, the owner of the she-ass and the owner of the mare.

At night, the king came, and he said to his wife: "I am the judge in this country, and you are the judge at home? You ate at home, you ate the food God granted you. Take whatever you want, take what is dearest to you, and go back to your father's house."

She said to him: "I will leave because a mare will never bear an ass."

Good, she waited for him to finish his supper, and then both he and she had some tea, and he went to sleep. The wife put a sleeping draught in the king's tea, and he drank it. He lost consciousness, fell to the floor, and slept. Alfahima sent for a carpenter. The carpenter arrived. She said to him: "Make a crate that has room for a mattress." He did so. He made the crate and put in the mattress and a pillow, and she put the king in the crate. She nailed the lid down and called four people, telling them to carry the crate to her father's house.

They did so, and her father was working, and her mother was busy. They were surprised and asked: "What about this crate, what about this crate she has sent us?" The crate was closed, they did not know what was inside.

The king's wife arrived along with the crate. She came to the house with the crate. They said to her: "What happened to this crate?" She said to them: "Something. Leave the crate here."

She stayed for the night. During the night, the king woke. He wanted to turn over, and he called his wife: "Alfahima!"

She said to him: "Yes."

He said to her: "What have you been doing to me?"

She said to him: "What do you mean? You told me 'Take what is dearest to you.' Is there anything in your house dearer to me than you? Nobody is dearer to me than you, and you said: 'Take what is most dear to you.' and that is what I did: I took you."

When he heard that, he was pleased. They sat down, they laughed, and his parents-in-law invited him to stay and were happy to have them. The next morning she returned with her husband. When they came to his house, she said: "What should be dearer to me in this house than you? You said to me: 'Take what is dearest to you,' and I took what is dearest to me."

## *Commentary:* IFA 16437

### QUEEN ALFAHIMA

The story belongs to the international type Aarne-Thompson 875: "The clever peasant girl" or, to be more precise, to part IV of Aarne-Thompson 875: "The dearest possession" and to Aarne-Thompson 875 E: "The unjust decision. The oil press gives birth to a colt." Narrative type Aarne-Thompson 875 is one of the most widespread folk narratives told by Jewish ethnic groups, and sixty-four parallel versions are deposited in the IFA.[1]

The opening of the story introduces the king's wife, Alfahima, who is characterized by a single trait—cleverness. This foreshadows the confrontation in the story, the confrontation between a husband

---

[1] The parallels are from different ethnic groups: Morocco, Tunisia, Libya, Egypt, Sefardi Israel, Syria, Yemen, Iraq, Persian Kurdistan, Persia, Bukhara, Afghanistan, Russia, and Poland.

A plate for Mimuna, a Jewish Moroccan folk festival. By kind permission of the Israel Museum, Jerusalem.

and his clever wife. For cleverness in a woman is not a trait given first priority in a patriarchal society. A certain Jewish folktale tells us that God first created a woman for man who was "more clever, more conniving, and more strong than man."[2] Thereupon, Adam spoke to God and said: "Please, God, I do not want this woman. Take her back, and give me another woman in her stead." And God created another woman for him who was beautiful, naive, and quiet, which implies that patriarchal society regards these as a woman's ideal qualities.

The first part of the story belongs solely to Aarne-Thompson 875 E. The king has to decide which of the two contending parties is right—the owner of the mare or the owner of the she-ass. He tries to show that he is clever and able to make a just decision, but he fails: his decision is blatantly unjust. To reprimand the king, his wife suggests that the owner of the mare, who had been wronged, should act and talk in an absurd manner. This would force the king to admit that the verdict he handed down was foolish. Enigmatic and absurd behavior occurs in folk narratives when a weak person must prove to a powerful person that he is wrong. Because the weak cannot correct the strong point-blank

---

[2] IFA 9584. Published in Shenhar 1974, no. 10.

without risking punishment, they must resort to stratagems to make the strong to admit their error without however punishing them. This is what happens in our story: in consequence of what the owner of the mare tells him, the king returns the colt, but he does not punish the man even though he was forced to overturn his verdict, for the king concluded that "as fish cannot eat cucumbers, so mares cannot foal asses."

However, the king knew that the stratagem employed by the owner of the mare had been suggested by his wife Alfahima. At this juncture, the confrontation (foreshadowed earlier) between the king and his clever wife develops, and the narrative that unfolds belongs to type Aarne-Thompson 875 part IV: "The dearest possession." This type, represented in the international folktale, also occurs in ancient Jewish literature, where it appears in several versions.[3] The confrontation is essentially sexual—between a man and a woman, and its purpose is to delimit woman's place and woman's status in a patriarchal society. The clever woman, who finds that her husband's decision is unjust, dares to violate a taboo inasmuch as she intervenes in the trial. We learn from the story that this is a valid reason for the husband to divorce his wife.

Because the story questions the role of women in patriarchal society, it is well liked by women. The protagonist is known for her cleverness that is, moreover, suggested by her name. She interferes in her husband's work, which is solely within his province, and she forces him to admit his error. Finally, she proves more clever than her husband when she (literally) carries out what he has told her to do, that is, to "take what is dearest to you and go back to your old home." She takes him to her parents' house and breaks a societal rule, which is that the married woman moves to her husband's house, and not the reverse.

However, the story, which is told in a patriarchal society, is no more than a statement: it does not attempt to change the order of society. The woman's reward is the return to her husband's house. The clever trick used by the woman—she takes him back home because he is dearest to her—moreover implies a compliment to the husband as well as an attempt at reconciliation; obviously the husband cannot help feeling flattered by her words and her actions.

It appears that in a traditional patriarchal society the right to

---

[3] The tale occurs as early as the Midrashic parable in Pesikta Rabati, Ish-Shalom Edition, 141; Pesikta De'rav Cahana, Mandelbaum Edition, 327; Song of Songs Raba A, B, Yalkut Shimoni, Bereshit, Siman 16; Midrash Hagadol Lekh Lekha 16c ("Get thee out of thy country"). Gaster 1968, no. 196. Cf. Noy 1972, no. 11 and note.

be angry is reserved to men, whereas conciliation is women's task. In this sense it is up to women to be wiser than their masters—men.

# Smeda Rmeda Who Was Turned into a Dove

### FROM: YAMNA DAYAN

It is told that God is everywhere. There was a rabbi, and as to this rabbi, he had a little daughter whose mother had borne her. At the end of two or three years, the mother died, and the girl lived. The girl grew up, and next to where she lived there lived a woman who had seven daughters, and this woman's husband was dead. The woman would stop the girl and take her to her house and comb her hair, wash her, dress her, wash her clothes, and do everything for her.

The girl kept growing, and the woman living next door would say: "Tell your father you want him to marry me."

The girl would talk to her father and say: "Father, this Jewess combed my hair, washed me with soap, washed my clothes and dressed me, and now I want you to marry no one but her."

He would say: "My daughter, when the year of mourning is over, and the year of joy begins we shall see who I am going to marry. The year of mourning for your mother will come to an end, and the year of joy will come, and we shall see who I am going to marry."

This is what she would tell him today, and this is what she would tell him tomorrow. Let's get on with the story. One day, one day they no longer felt the anxiety caused by the mother's death. At the end of the year of mourning they performed a ceremony to commemorate the day she had passed on, and they were free from the anxiety they had felt when she died, and he married the neighbor and did not take in any one of her daughters; he only took in the mother.

He took in the mother. This Jew loved his daughter dearly. She was as dear to him as his own soul.

She [the neighbor] became his wife, but the daughter was not ready to part with her father. She would sleep with him, sharing his bed; she would urinate on him and relieve herself. He would say to her, to the woman: "This is my daughter; we won't separate."

## Smeda Rmeda Who Was Turned into a Dove

One day, what did the rabbi's wife do? She prepared hummus[1] for supper, and she took several handfuls of salt and added them to the chick-peas, and she said to him: "This is what your daughter is going to eat, and this is what she is going to drink."

The father was not present. And she gave her bowls of chick-peas, one after the other. Let's get on with the story.

The next morning she filled their bed with excrement. She said to him: "And now—are you going to allow your daughter to spend the night with you? And then you go to synagogue to pray—and you being a rabbi? Look at the bed, look at what she did to the bed, look at the clothes, look what she has done to them."

He said to her: "What are we going to do to her?"

She said to him: "You ask me what we are going to do to her. Let's go and get a cage, let's send her to the kitchen, and let's put her into the cage there. We will give her food and drink there, in the cage."

He went off and took the girl to the kitchen and put her into the cage, and she [the step-mother] would give her food and drink. Let's get on with the story—day in, day out, day in, day out. And let it be said: the girl grew up and turned into a young woman as beautiful as a roe-deer. But the poor thing had her food there and her drink there, and she relieved herself there.

One day the king wanted to have a banquet.[2] He sent for the rabbi and his wife; he wanted them to be present. Then the rabbi said to his wife: "Oh my daughter, the king is my friend, I visit him and I spend time with him, and now we have to go and see him."

She said to him: "I and my daughters, we have nothing to wear, we have no clothes, and we have no shoes, we have nothing."

He turned to the eldest daughter, and he said: "You come here. What do you want?" And then he turned to the next daughter and he said: "Come here. What do you want?" . . . Shoes, dresses—until he had given them everything.

As they were leaving the house he remembered, and he said: "Oh dear, now in connection with that poor girl—I forgot her. Let's go and see what she would like to have."

He went to the kitchen, and he said to her: "My daughter, what can I get you? Maybe you too want something."

She said to him: "Father, don't bring me anything. Just bring me six nuts. Six nuts."

---

[1] A dish prepared from chick-peas. It is a very popular food in the Mediterranean countries.

[2] A banquet to choose a bride.

Now the story goes like this: he left; he traveled to a big city. He bought them shoes. He bought them belts. He bought them clothes; he bought them everything. And again, he forgot his own daughter. When the market was empty, and he was about to leave, he said: "Oh dear, and the girl—I haven't bought her the six nuts." He returned to the market, and there was just one man there, and this man had a saddlebag full of nuts.

He said to him: "Sell me ten nuts, or twenty, or thirty."

He said to him: "I am not going to open the saddlebag to sell you ten nuts, or thirty nuts, no matter what you pay me. If you like, you can take the whole bag. If not, just leave. The market is empty, and I am on my way."

He said to him: "Alright."

He sold him the saddlebag. He sold it to him, and he carried it off.

Now the story goes like this: he put it on the back of his mule, and as he was driving the mule, the nuts dropped to the ground because there was a hole in the bag, they kept dropping, dropping, dropping, dropping—till there were just six nuts left, the six nuts the girl had asked for.

He came home, and when he unloaded the bag he found it was empty.

He started saying: "Oh dear, oh dear, oh dear, what am I going to do about this girl, the poor thing, I have not brought her anything." He started rummaging in the bag, first in one corner and then in another, until finally he found the six nuts she had asked for. He took the six nuts, put them in his pocket, picked up the saddlebag and stepped into the room. He brought in the suitcase containing the clothes, and he said to each of the girls; "You take this, and you take that, and you take that." And they were busy putting the clothes on, and busy washing, and he walked into the kitchen to speak to his daughter. He said to her: "Take these. I brought you a saddlebag full of nuts, but they dropped to the ground because there was a hole in the bag, and I did not notice it, and they fell on the ground. Here, take the six nuts you yourself asked for. This is what is left."

She said to him: "Alright, father."

He gave the girl the nuts, and the rest of the family finished putting on the clothes, and the demon, his wife, she took a sack of flour, a sack of grain, a sack of chick-peas, and a sack of corn, emptied them on the floor and mixed them, and said to the girl: "Mind you, when I come back here tonight and I don't find the contents of the sacks sorted, with each grain where it belongs, you don't know what I am going to do to you."

The poor thing wept, and nobody took any notice of her. Good—now she was getting ready to sort over the contents of the six sacks. The girl said: "Good—I trust in God." They had left; they had locked her inside the house; they were gone. She got out the nuts. She ate the first nut. She got out the second nut, and she ate it. She said: "I am going to eat the nuts, and I am going to trust in God. And I am going to sort over the contents of the sacks." Let's get on with the story. She kept eating the nuts till just one nut was left. As she was cracking that nut, He appeared. He stood next to her; he said to her: "What is it you wish, Madam? Madam, what do you want? What does Her Ladyship wish?"

She said to him: "What does Your Ladyship want? What is it Madam wants? Sort over the contents of all these sacks for me. Put everything where it belongs. Put everything into the right sack. Then sew the sacks up and stack them one on top of the other. Then come back here so I can tell you what I want."

He started working. Now the story goes like this: he finished sorting at once. He said to her: "Close your eyes, and then open them again." She closed her eyes and opened them again. She saw that everything had been sorted over. The sacks were sewn up and stacked. He said to her: "What is it you want?"

She said to him: "I want a green dress, and a green horse, and slippers, and I want the slippers to be green to match the dress. And take me to the seven daughters of my father's wife and leave me there."

He said to her: "Alright." He gave her green shoes. The shoes were studded with gold all over. He gave her a green dress, and green shoes, and a green horse, and everything she needed. Then he sat her down among the seven daughters who were being entertained by the king.

Now the youngest daughter stood up and walked over to her mother. She said to her: "Smeda Rmeda, the one who destroys her luck with her own hands, she is here."

She said to her: "Come off it, you may have worse to tell. Is it conceivable that a filthy girl whose own excrement is all over her body should come here, to the king's palace?"

She replied: "If this is not Smeda Rmeda who destroys her luck with her own hands you may kill me."

She spoke to her sisters, and they walked up to Smeda Rmeda one by one and looked at her. Their mother said to them: "It is not her. Where should she get such a dress from? Not even you have dresses like that, and you have money. How should a girl who lives in her own filth be able to look like this?"

Fine. They kept quiet. They held their tongues. Smeda Rmeda said to the genie: "Don't be late. The moment you see the party is over come back for me and take me to my cage. In the meantime wash my clothes, clean my cage, scrub it and tidy it up, and then come back for me and put me in the cage."

He washed her clothes, dried and folded them and put them in the cage. He washed the cage and put it straight, and then he picked her up. As he was carrying her back—as he was running very fast, very fast—as he was crossing the spring where the king's horses were watered—on the way—she dropped one of her slippers. The slipper fell into the spring. He changed her clothes, and he returned her to her cage, quietly, silently.

They returned home at night. The mother said to her daughter: "Didn't I tell you? Where would Smeda Rmeda ever get a dress like that from? And if she had gotten such a dress, she would have stayed there. She would not have come back here."

The younger daughter (may she be unlucky) replied: "It's no good, mother. It was her. If it wasn't her, kill me."

The mother replied: "My daughter, you are very dear to me. But how could she ever get a dress like that? And who would take her out of the cage? Who would escort her? Where would she get such a horse from? Where?"

The girl said to the other members of the family: "I told you it was her. You will see."

The next day they took the horses to the spring, but they would not drink. They hung their heads, and they saw the shoe in the water, shining, for it was all gold. And they would not drink. They would not drink today, and they would not drink tomorrow, the same thing today, and the same thing tomorrow. For eight or ten days. The horses were dying of thirst. They went to see the king. They said to him: "Your Majesty, put your hand on your head and say 'May they be forgiven.'"

He said to them: "God will forgive you if you tell the truth."

They said to the king: "Your Majesty, the horses we have been trying to water for the past eight days are going to die of thirst. Three thousand or four thousand horses crowd around the spring and lower their heads to drink, and we do not know what they see in the water, and then they raise up their heads and move away."

The king said to them: "Now then, what are we going to do?"

They replied: "Send for the chief counsellor and the counsellors and ask them to tell you what you should do."

He sent for the chief counsellor. The counsellors arrived, and he said to them: "What do you suggest I should do about those horses that have been refusing to drink water from the spring for eight days on end? All the horses are about to die. Three or four thousand horses—they lower their heads to drink water from the spring, and then they see whatever they see, and they turn about and go back home."

The counsellors asked: "Are there any divers? Tell the divers to look. There probably is a snake there, or a viper, or a human being who fell into the water and died, and this is what frightens them, or something like that."

They sent for divers, and the divers searched the pool. They search, and lo and behold, they find the shoe. They bring the shoe to the king's son who was standing there next to them. The king's son said: "Oh, what a beautiful shoe! Look at the shoe, and imagine the lovely owner who had worn it. Lead the horses back to the stables." They did so. He said to them: "Issue a proclamation. No woman is allowed to stay home. All the women must come and try on the shoe. I shall marry the one whose foot fits the shoe." (You see, that's what happens when God wants to make someone happy.)

Now the story goes on like this: the king's son kept a record. Using a pencil and a notebook, he wrote down the names of all those whose foot was measured against the shoe. This one's foot was measured, and that one's foot was measured, and this one's foot was measured, and that one's foot was measured. Finally they heard about it in the palace of the king's father. Another proclamation was issued, and more feet were measured, and at that point the step-mother with her seven daughters went [to the palace] to have their feet measured against the shoe. She was very pleased: Maybe the shoe would fit her daughter's foot. They all went [to the palace]; there was not a single one that stayed behind. Policemen came and searched the rooms: perhaps there was one [girl] who did not have her foot measured. And they found that poor thing, the girl in the cage. And a certain member of the search party said: "Am I really to take her to the king's palace? She is filthy all over. What am I to do so I can take her to the palace?"

He went off. He said to the king: "Your Majesty, there is nobody left. There is just one girl—it would be beneath your dignity to meet with her. They keep her in a cage, and she is filthy, and you would not want to see her."

He said to the policeman: "Get her. I swore no woman would be left out."

He went off. Now the story goes on like this: he drew water from the well, he washed her hands and her feet, and even though she was covered with filth he led her to the palace. When she tried on the shoe, it fitted her like a glove.

The king said to the policemen and to the search party: "Tell them to hand her over to the nurse and her assistants, and tell the nurse to take the girl to the public bath-house and to bathe her, to perfume her, and to give her a dress that befits her beauty because I want to marry her."

So far, so good. Now the catty little girl stood up and said: "Didn't I tell you, didn't I tell you this was Smeda Rmeda who brings misfortune upon herself?"

They almost died, so furious were they. She and her daughters. But the rabbi, that poor man, he was happy, happy he got rid of that filth and all that.

So far, so good. The king's son married her, and there was a big wedding, but none but God is great. He invited all the town, he slaughtered cattle, he slaughtered oxen, he slaughtered all kinds (of animals), and he made the biggest wedding feast ever.

Fine. She sat next to him, they laughed, they played games, they were not short on anything. One day, her father's wife stands up and turns to her youngest daughter, and she says: "Come, go and see the one who dirties her clothes. See how she is doing. See if she is the way she used to be, or whether she has settled in at the king's."

The youngest daughter set out and brought her gifts. What did she bring? She brought bread; she brought meat. She visited her and brought her bread, and brought her everything. They were sitting and talking, sitting and talking, and she gave her seven blind needles.[3] And the mother said to the youngest daughter: "If you meet her, ask her to let you examine her scalp, to find out whether anything is left of what she had [on her scalp] when she was kept in the cage.[4] And then you stick the seven blind needles into her head, and she will turn into a dove and fly off. And you put on her clothes and sit down, and when the king comes, you greet him with a smile, and talk to him, and he will not notice anything."

She left, so the story goes. The gatekeeper let her in, and she greeted the king's wife. She sat down next to her, and she offered her

---

[3] A needle without an eye.

[4] When a person wanted to show that he or she liked someone, it was customary— especially for women—for him or her to examine the other person's hair for lice.

bread, and she offered her roast meat, and they ate and drank. The girl said to the king's wife: "Let me have a look at your head." (The king had not yet arrived.) "Let me have a look at your head. Do you still have lice, the way you used to have lice when you were inside the cage?"

As she was examining the girl's hair, she stuck the seven pins into her head. The girl turned into a dove, and she flew off. Her step-sister put on her clothes and sat down in the queen's chair. The king's son came in. He did not feel attracted to the girl. He stared at her, and that was all.

He did not know what to do: should he talk or should he keep quiet? But when the queen—the dove—saw that the king had come in, she flew over a low wall, and, facing him, she said:

My father gave me things,
and my mother deceived me.
The king's son took me,
and he was kind to me,
and he gave me things.
Her daughter came and deceived me.
Oh trees,
Be my witness. Weep over me!
You stones, weep!
Oh you son of the king,
weep for me at the gate of my palace.

And when the dove flew away, the wall across which she had come in collapsed. The next day they rebuilt the wall, and at lunchtime the dove recited the same verses again. Let's get on with the story. Let's get on with the story.

One day, the king's son decided to speak to the chief counsellor. He said: "Chief counsellor, what do you suggest I should do? There is a certain dove which says this, and which says that. When I rebuild the wall, she comes and recites her verses, and when she flies away the wall collapses again."

The counsellor replied: "This time you must tar the wall. When the dove wants to fly away, her feet will stick to the tar and then you can catch her and find out what she wants to tell you."

Now the story goes on like this: he rebuilt the wall, and he tarred it. She came, and she again recited the same verses. When she wanted to fly away, her feet were stuck. The king's son caught the dove, and he said: "What a beautiful dove, what a beautiful dove, what a beautiful dove."

He fondled the dove's head, and as he was doing so, touched

141

A bag for pregnant women. By kind permission of the Israel Museum, Jerusalem.

the seven needles. He pulled out the first needle, he pulled out the second needle, he pulled out the third needle and the fourth and so on, until there was only one needle left. The moment he pulled out that needle, the dove was turned into his wife. He said to her: "Where have you been?"

She said to him: "Where have I been? Where have I been?"

He said to her: "Who did this to you?"

She replied: "That sister of mine on my father's side, she is the one who did that to me."

He said to her: "And now, what do you decide in connection with her?"

She said to him: "What do I decide? I'll cut her to pieces, but my blood won't stop boiling. I want you to hand her over to the people so they can trample her down into the ground for seven days, till she turns into powdery flour. Then my blood will stop boiling, and my fury will subside."

Now the story goes on like this: he sent for his policemen, and they beat her, and then they slaughtered her. They cut her body into four pieces, first they cut off the arms and then they cut off the legs, and then they cut off the head, and they stuffed the pieces into a sack, and handed the sack to the guard, and she said: "Take this to her mother and tell her 'this is the gift the king's wife sent you.'"

Fine. Now the story goes on like this: he took the gift to her mother. Now, when the girl had turned the queen into a dove and

142

had taken her place, she had filled a sack with dates, raisins, and almonds and so on which she sent to her mother. And now she was sending her little daughter, slaughtered, and cut into four pieces and wrapped up in a sack.

Good. She sent the sack to the mother. The mother was very pleased, and she called her neighbors, and she said to them: "Oh neighbors, see what my daughter has sent me. Last time she sent me a sack full of dates, raisins, nuts, and almonds, but this time she is sending me roast meat and bread."

Then she opened the pathetic sack and found her daughter's head lying face up on top of the dismembered body. Then the mother said to her neighbors: "All those who have shared food with me should come and share my grief. Those who have shared food with me should share my grief with me now."

The neighbors came, all those who had laughed and rejoiced when she had given them the Elfakya[5] her daughter had sent her, and now they wept with her.

And the tale flows on with the rivers
And our friends are generous givers.

## Commentary: IFA 14566

### SMEDA RMEDA WHO TURNED INTO A DOVE

This narrative is another version of the Cinderella tale of Moroccan Jews, and it belongs to Aarne-Thompson 510 A. A different version narrated by Freha Ḥafuta is also included in this book (see above); that earlier commentary deals with most elements recurring in the present narrative. But we felt that Yamna Dayan's version should be included, too; not only is it a work of art in its own right, but also the two narratives represent the two basic Moroccan-Jewish versions of this folk narrative.[1]

As the earlier narrative has been exhaustively treated, we focus here on a few special features of this version only.

As distinct from the earlier narrative in which Smeda Rmeda kills her own mother, there is no matricide in this narrative. The saying "Smeda Rmeda who destroys her luck with her own hands," which features in all Moroccan-Jewish Cinderella narratives, refers

---

[5] A mixture of raisins, nuts, almonds, and so on.

[1] For an exhaustive treatment of the Smeda Rmeda narrative, see Bar-Itzhak 1992.

to the fact that she herself persuaded her father to marry the neighbor, who later causes her suffering and misery. The two elements— matricide committed at the instigation of the woman who wants the father, and the father's marriage to another woman as a result of pressure put on him by his own daughter—are typical features of narratives presented in a Muslim context. Presumably, these two features derive from this context (Bar-Itzhak 1992). Most Jewish versions from Asia and Africa contain this feature.[2] In the version quoted by Margaret Mills from the Muslim-Persian culture, a version she claims is characteristic of Persia and Afghanistan, two elements occur. First, merchant enrolls his daughter in a religious school; the teacher is a widow who questions the girl about the financial standing of her family. When she learns that they are well off, she convinces the girl that she is well disposed to her, as distinct from her mother who dislikes her. She then suggests that the girl should push the mother into a vat of vinegar, which is stored in their house, and put the lid on. The girl does so, and sometime later the father marries the teacher. The teacher bears a daughter of her own and starts maltreating the step-daughter (Mills 1982, 183–185).

Second, the oedipal elements, expressed by the father's refusal to distance himself from his daughter as well as the element of excretion without restraint, are more explicitly presented in the version of this narrator than in the version narrated by Freha Hafuta, for the narrator uses the words: "She used to sleep with him in his bed; she used to urinate on him and relieve herself all over him."

The two narratives are also similar in that both have a supernatural helper, a genie who emerges from a nut. They differ in that there is only one genie in our narrative but several in the other version. The fact that Smeda Rmeda wants the genie to give her green clothes is a symbolic expression of her wish to get married and serves as an anticipating motif in the narrative plot. This is to be understood against the background of tradition that prescribed the dress of Moroccan-Jewish brides should be green, the color symbolizing fertility.

The shoe test is equally included in both versions. However, a dramatic dimension is added as the shoe is dropped and falls into the well from which the horses refuse to drink. This subplot delays the main plot and adds suspense.

In this narrative, too, the wedding does not conclude the narra-

---

[2] IFA has sixteen versions from other Islamic countries, viz. Tunisia, Turkey, Lebanon, Sefardi Israel, Yemen, Iraqi Kurdistan, Persian Kurdistan, Iraq, Bukhara, and Afghanistan.

tive plot. This is a characteristic feature of the Smeda Rmeda narrative in general (Bar-Itzhak 1992). The girl endures more misery when she is turned into a dove while the step-sister pretends she is the wife. We therefore deal with a conglomerate of Aarne-Thompson 510 A and Aarne-Thompson 403 IV: "The substituted bride."

The main difference between this narrative and Freha Hafuta's version is the transformation where the girl turns into a dove. This motif is absent in Freha's version where the protagonist is pushed down a well. In this narrative the mother gives her daughter seven blind needles and tells her to clean Smeda Rmeda's hair and to stick the needles into her head. When she does so, Smeda Rmeda is turned into a dove, which flies off, escaping through an open window. But the dove persists, and the song she sings leads to her discovery. Her husband removes the needles, and she is transformed into his true wife.

This version is a conglomerate of three narrative types: Aarne-Thompson 510 A—"Cinderella"; Aarne-Thompson 403 IV "The substituted bride"—onto which Aarne-Thompson 405 is added— "Jorinde and Joringel (chiefly motif D 154.1: "A human being is turned into a dove"). Here a magician turns a girl into a bird, and a young man helped by a spell restores her to her former self.

# The Clever Girl

FROM: YAMNA DAYAN

A Hakham had no children, and then he had a daughter of superb beauty. She was a clever girl, too, before something happened she would anticipate it. Let's get on with the story, let's get on.

The king heard about this girl.

They said: "The Hakham has had a daughter, and that daughter is clever. Whatever is going to happen in this world—she foresees it."

The king rose and said: "I will send emissaries to the Hakham, and he will give her to me in marriage."

He sent his emissaries, and they said to him: "The king wants you to send him your daughter so he can marry her."

In those days everything belonged to the Jews; the king was a Jew; and everybody was Jewish.

They arrived, and they told him.

The Ḥakham replied: "I will be glad to give her to the king."

Good, the king went out, and he bought two slaves, and he sent her gifts. He sent her everything for the betrothal. Six or seven jars of honey, some sheep, some velvet, some brocade, the most expensive kind, and he told the slaves to go to her house and deliver the gifts.

They went there, and they knocked on the door.

She said to them: "Who knocks on the woman of valor without asking?"

They said to her: "The master's servants."

She said to them: "But there is no one to open the door."

They said to her: "And what of you?"

She said to them: "Me—my reason is in my lap."

They said to her: "And what of your mother?"

She said to them: "She is out. She is taking away a woman's pregnancy."

They said to her: "And what of your father?"

She said to them: "He is out. He is serving his lord."

—"And what of your brother?"

—"He went to the loss market. Climb over the mason's wall and come down the carpenter's wall and enter."

They did so. They climbed over the top of the door and slid down the wall and entered.

Good. She rose, and washed her hands, and extended her hospitality to them. She accepted the gifts they had brought.

She said to them: "Tell the king: 'by the souls of your grandfathers, you must not harm the two slaves:

> For the sea is short of two pitchers
> And the sky is short of two yards.
> The horns are there
> But two pairs are missing.'"

The slaves left, laughing. They said: "Really . . . she is crazy. And the king wants to marry her?"

Good, and she calls after them: "Swear that you will say to the king 'Swear by the souls of your grandfathers . . .' and report everything to him."

They, left and they did so. They came to the king's house; they bowed; they kissed his thigh.

He said to them: "What happened? Did she receive you?"

—"Sir, put your hand on our heads and say 'May they be forgiven.'"

A mortar and a pestle, still in use in Shlomi.

He said to them: "May God forgive you, if you tell the truth."
They said to him: "That girl, she seems like crazy."
He said to them: "Why? Did she beat you?"
They said to him: "No, no, she did not beat us at all, we just knocked on the door. 'She said to us:

Who knocks on the woman of valor?
Who knocks on the serious-minded girls
and does not ask their permission?'

We said to her: 'The master's servants.'
She said to us: 'Good, there is no one here to open the door.'
We said to her: 'Why? And what of you?'
She said to us: 'Me? My reason is in my lap.'
We said to her: 'And what of your mother?'
She said to us: 'She is taking away a woman's pregnancy.'
　　　　—'And your father?'
She said to us: 'He went to serve his lord.'
　　　　—'And your brother?'
　　　　—'He went to the loss market.'
And finally she said to us: 'Tell the king: By the souls of his grandfathers, he must not hurt the two slaves

For the sea is short of two pitchers
And the sky is short of two yards.

The horns are there
But two pairs are missing.'"

He said to them: "Good, go, go to her house and return what you stole. I may be tired, or I may not be tired, but I would have cut off your flesh and roasted it and make you eat it but for the fact that she will not let me do so. I trusted you with the gifts, and you committed theft. You are foolish, you did not understand anything. Her mother is a midwife, she was delivering a baby. Her brother was gambling; her father went to the synagogue to pray; and she was combing her hair, and that is why her reason was in her lap. Now you go there, and return the two pitchers and the material and the two sheep."

Good, the girl came and married the king. They made a big wedding feast, and none is as great as God.

And the story flows with the rivers
And our friends are generous givers.

## Commentary: IFA 16438

### The Clever Girl

The narrative belongs to Aarne-Thompson 875 A: "Girl's riddling answer betrays a theft." In the majority of folk-narratives of Jewish ethnic groups this narrative combines two narrative plots. It forms a conglomerate consisting of Aarne-Thompson 875: "The clever peasant girl"[1] and especially Aarne-Thompson 875 part IV: "The dearest possession."[2] The combination is not in this narrative, although the opening is suggestive of its narration by Moroccan Jews.[3] For the most part, the narrative deals with a girl whose father had wanted a son and, being angry about the birth of a girl, refuses to give her a name. When the girl grows up, she calls herself the cleverest of maidens. After a time, the king asks the father riddles. The daughter is the one to know the answers, and when the king finds out about it, he wants to marry her, and sends messengers who bring her gifts. The plot of our narrative starts at this point. As the part

---

[1] Sixty-four narratives of this type are preserved in the IFA. They were recorded from the following Jewish ethnic groups: Morocco, Tunisia, Libya, Egypt, Israel Sefardi, Syria, Yemen, Iraq, Kurdistan, Persia, Bukhara, Afghanistan, Russia, and Poland.

[2] See "Queen Alfahima" (narrative and commentary) above.

[3] Cf. the narrative published in Shenhar and Bar-Itzhak 1981, 145–154.

of the plot leading up to this point is absent, it is presented as a generalization by the narrator who explains that the king wants to marry the girl because of her beauty and mainly because of her sharp mind and ability to anticipate events that are to occur in the future. The narrative plot centers on the enigmatic utterances of the girl who gives the king's emissaries messages that they convey to the king without understanding their import. This type of narrative is an intellectual challenge to the listeners. They try to find the answers to the girl's riddles, and for the most part they understand their meanings before the king gives the answers (i.e., the listener solve the riddles on the plot level). Thus, the narrative makes the listeners feel superior to the messengers, the foolish protagonists of the narrative who convey the girl's messages to the king, unaware of the fact that they bring about their own destruction. The interpretations suggested by the king reinforce and complement the answers of the listeners, and on the plot level they show the messengers that they have done something foolish and that they have to return the stolen gifts.

The genre of this folk narrative is the novella of cleverness. On the overt level it appears as though the main confrontation is between the clever girl and the foolish messengers who try to steal the king's gifts, but on the covert level the confrontation is on a sexual basis, between the king and his future wife. The role of riddles in wedding ceremonies and in narratives about weddings has been exhaustively treated by Dov Noy (1973). Noy pointed out that the riddle is an expression of sublimation of the struggle prior to the wedding when the future husband and wife try to discover the character and personality of their respective partners. They do not ask each other riddles, but rather have the riddles as well as the presents conveyed by messengers. This oriental approach defers the meeting of the partners in marriage till after the wedding.

The narrative is a feminine novella: it reflects the aspirations of women in a patriarchal society. The girl is clever: she asks the riddles, and it is up to the man to make an effort and find the answers to prove he deserves her and is not inferior to his future wife. In most narratives the plot of Aarne-Thompson 875 part IV: "The dearest possession" is introduced at this point. Here the girl is ready to marry the man on condition that should he hurt her she will be permitted to take possession of what is dearest to her in her husband's house and return to her parents' house. When the husband does in fact hurt her, she puts him to sleep and has him transported to her parents' house. Thus she demonstrates that she is indeed superior inasmuch as she was able to anticipate the future. Moreover, she proves to be a woman of wisdom because her conduct appeases the husband who no longer has any cause to be displeased with a wife to whom he is the dearest thing in the world. In this narrative this final segment is not included, and the two characters get married the moment the king solves the riddles and the messengers return the stolen property.

# Yoseph Peretz

WHEN WE recorded the folktales Yoseph Peretz was more than eighty years old. He was born in Marakesh, where his father Shlomo and his mother Hanina were living.

In the old country, Yoseph produced a special cotton thread that is used to weave the traditional long robe worn by the Arabs. Yoseph was childless, but his wife Suleika-ben-Simon, whom he married thirty-five years ago had children. When we recorded him Yoseph was hospitalized in a Home for the Aged, owing to illness and old age. His wife's children, who were close to him, helped us to record the story of his background.

Yoseph heard folk narratives in his country of origin, especially from friends. He, too, would tell folk narratives whenever he was asked to do so. He would mainly narrate his folk narratives in the synagogue and at the club for old-age pensioners when his friends were there.

His family testified that they found his narratives interesting and that they were sorry they were unable to continue enjoying them.

# *Who Is Unclean?*

### From: Yoseph Peretz

There was a king, and there was a rabbi who lived in the king's house. And the king loved the rabbi; the rabbi was his closest friend. Anything the rabbi did not do, the king did not do.

The minister rose and said to the king: "The Jew drops by every hour, bends down and kisses you . . . after all, you are a king. Is it right for a Jew to bend down and kiss you?[1] You ought to humble him."

The minister was envious of the rabbi, and when a minister is envious, my friends,[2] the rabbi gets hurt.

The rabbi went to his wife and said to her: "Oh woman, the king does not relate to me the way he used to relate to me in the past. And now give me the string of pearls you are wearing around your neck."

He removed one pearl and took it to the king's house, but instead of giving it to the king's wife, he gave it to a servant girl. The servant girl went and showed it to her mistress, the king's wife.

She said to her: "Look, this pearl was given to me by the Ḥazzan.[3] That is how he honored me."

They liked this servant, and the king allowed her to keep the pearl.

When the rabbi came, the king said to him: "Ḥazzan, you committed two errors."

He said to him: "What errors, Sir?"

He said to him: "You gave a pearl to a servant girl, but my wife, the king's wife—you did not give her a pearl."

He said to him: "Sir, I will tell you the truth. God wanted mankind to have two pearls, one was lowered into our world by Our Lord Mohammed, and the minister took it, and the other was lowered into our world by Our Lord Moses, and I took it. I wanted to give it

---

[1] He implies that by touching the Jew, the king becomes unclean; see commentary.

[2] The narrator is addressing the audience.

[3] Muslims usually call rabbis "Ḥazzan."

to your wife, but when I entered her room, I lowered my eyes, and I do not know to whom I gave that pearl."

He said to him: "Very nice," and sent for the minister.

He said to him: "Look, this Ḥazzan, whom you have discredited, he brought this pearl to the palace, and you took it and did not hand it over. Now go and bring the pearl to my wife."

The minister went to the rabbi. He brought him sheep; he brought him presents so he should save him.

The rabbi said to him: "Two costly pearls were in our possession; one fell into the sewer, and the other—I took it to the king. And now, if you want the pearl, go down into the sewer and start looking for it."

He said to him: "Bring laborers, and pay them any price they ask."

He said to him: "No matter what laborer you hire—when he finds the pearl in the sewer, he will swallow it and come up and say: 'I did not find it!' The only way for you to succeed is by doing it yourself!"

The luckless minister took off his silken clothes, his robes and his gowns, and climbed down into the sewer. He put on a sack and emptied the sewer.

The rabbi called the king.

He said: "Come and look at the minister, just see where he is."

The king came, he lifted the curtain, and there is the minister—in the sewer.

He said to him: "Now who is unclean, the Ḥazzan or you? Come up, come up, come straight up."

The minister came up, may God spare us such humiliation, put on his clothes and came before the king.

The king said to him: "The property of the minister will go to the rabbi, and he [the minister] will no longer be a minister. And the minister's dwelling will go to the rabbi, and he [the rabbi] will live there."

—"Now," the rabbi said to him, "just look at the one who told you that I make you unclean if I come and kiss your shoulders. And now, who is unclean, he or I? Who is unclean?"

Grave stones from South Morocco. By kind permission of the Israel Museum, Jerusalem.

## Commentary: IFA 16456

### WHO IS UNCLEAN?

Typologically, this folktale can be assigned to Aarne-Thompson 837: "How The Wicked Lord Was Punished",[1] to Aarne-Thompson 1528*D (IFA): "Contest in cleverness between Jew and gentile; Jew wins",[2] and to Aarne-Thompson 922*E: "The visit to Mecca."[3]

This folktale deals with a confrontation between two religions. The genre to which it belongs is the novella of deceit in which the Jew comes out the winner because he is able to pull a clever trick on the king and his minister. The trick is presented as enigmatic

---

[1] In IFA, eighteen versions of Aarne-Thompson 739 are recorded: Morocco (1) (in Noy 1964, no. 46), Libya (1) (Noy 1967, no. 62), Egypt (1), Turkey (1) (Stahl 1976, no. 10), Israel Sefardi (3), Israel Ashkenazi (1), Iraqi Kurdistan (1), Iraq (2), Rumania (2), Poland (3), Lithuania (2) (Noy 1963b, no. 17).

[2] In IFA, forty-four versions of Aarne-Thompson 1528*D are recorded: Morocco (4), Tunisia (2) (in Noy 1972, no. 12), Egypt (1), Yugoslavia (1), Lebanon (1), Israel Sefardi (5), Israel Ashkenazi (2), Yemen (7), Iraqi Kurdistan (3), Iraq (8), Persia (2) (in Mizrahi 1967, no. 34), Afghanistan (1), Poland (3), Russia (3) (in Baharav 1968, nos. 38, 39), Lithuania (1).

[3] In IFA, five versions of this type are recorded: Morocco (1) (in Noy 1964, no. 35), Tunisia (1), Egypt (1) (in Noy 1963b, no. 90), Yemen (1), Afghanistan (1).

behavior: not only the other characters, but also the listeners cannot, at first, discover linkages between the rabbi's actions and the change in the king's treatment of him. "Oh woman, the king does not treat me as he used to treat me in the past. And now, hand your string of pearls over to me." Initially, the fact that the gift is given to the servant girl is equally enigmatic; only when the rabbi talks to the king do the listeners understand that his keen mind had presaged the king's reaction and that he had therefore chosen to give the pearl to the servant.

The trick serves a twofold purpose: it revitalizes the king's friendship for the rabbi, and it allows the rabbi to pay the minister back.

What the minister charges the rabbi with (that he is unclean), is a serious accusation, for it is leveled at his Jewishness. It is serious because Judaism lays special emphasis on purity as distinct from its opposite, profaneness. But it also pinpoints the Muslim belief that Jews are the profane people because they do not believe in Muhammad. To pay the minister back, the Jew must therefore direct the punishment to precisely the same area in which he himself had been degraded.

The narrator obviously derives pleasure from the thought of the minister's defilement. It should be borne in mind that folktales such as this one were generated in a hostile environment where the persecuted Jewish minority was held in contempt. In these folktales, which are structured like the Book of Esther, the Jews probably found solace and an outlet for the hatred that had accumulated over the centuries.

# JULIETTE MEGERA

**WHEN WE** recorded the folktales, Juliette Megera was forty-five years old. She came from the town of Safi in Morocco, where her parents lived. Their names were Meir Alkasalsi and Pirha. She was educated in an Alliance Israelite Universelle school in Morocco,[1] was married in 1952, and came to Israel in 1955.

When they first came, the family was sent to Shomera, where there were some twenty families, none of whom was Moroccan. The settlement had neither electricity nor water. Juliette and her husband, who were used to an urban environment, refused to live in a settlement, and they finally went to Shlomi because another family from their town was living there. Juliette's husband served as the clerk of the local council for about sixteen years and was then appointed a director of the Amidar Housing Project. Juliette is a housewife. She has eleven children and seven grandchildren, some of whom were serving in the Israel Defence Force.

---

[1] The name of the story-teller and the name of the woman protagonist in her narrative are pointing to the influence of French culture on Jews in Morocco, especially on those who were educated in the Alliance schools.

Juliette heard her family tell folk narratives when she was living in the old country, and in Israel too she heard folk narratives on holidays and special occasions, and she herself would narrate folktales, especially when traveling "to pass the time." According to her, people were always ready to listen to her narratives.

# *The Story of Rabbi Ḥaim Pinto*

FROM: JULIETTE MEGERA

The son of Rabbi Ḥaim Pinto was married to my cousin, and when their first son was born, they named him Ḥaim Pinto, after his grandfather.[1]

When the child was one year old, he died. He died on the eve of the Sabbath.

The woman wanted to cry and to wail. Her husband, Moses, came and told her: "I don't want you to cry or wail or do anything connected with mourning. Take the child to the room and put him in his cradle, and close the door. Leave the room and do [what is necessary] to honor the Sabbath.

The woman trusted her husband, who came from a family of pious and righteous men. She went out and prepared the Sabbath, they recited the blessing over the wine and over the bread and the Havdala and the prayer, till they finished all of it.

Her mother came, she asked: "Where is the child?"

She said to her: "The child—the servant took him for a little walk for a good time because he would not let us sit quietly at the table."

The next morning the husband rose again and went to the synagogue, and the wife set the table as usual.

He came home from the synagogue, blessed the food and ate dinner, left again for the afternoon prayers, and went out again for the evening prayers. At night she prepared the Havdala[2] at the end

---

[1] It is a custom among Sefardi and Middle Eastern Jews to name children also after living grandparents.

[2] A ceremony performed when the Sabbath ends to distinguish between holy and secular.

of the Sabbath, and they laid the table as usual. She served him food till the Sabbath ended, he blessed the wine.

At night, when they lit the lights again, he called her and said: "Madeleine, now you may go to the room and see your child."

She entered the room and found her son alive, crying in the cradle.

She was overjoyed; she left the room and said to him: "Moses, the child was dead yesterday, and look—today he is alive."

He said to her: "Do you know why he was brought back to life? Thanks to my father and thanks to the Sabbath, which you did not spoil, and because you as always did all that is necessary for the Sabbath. Thanks to that the child is alive."

The child, who was brought back to life, became a scholar and a rabbi and he married the daughter of Rabbi Yitzhak Abu-Ḥatzera, whose family live in Netivot.

He took his wife to Canada and became a great rabbi there, and he had children, everything thanks to his father and grandfather, who were great rabbis.

## *Commentary:* IFA 16449

### THE STORY OF RABBI ḤAIM PINTO

The narrator heard this tale from her mother, and she herself narrates it on various occasions. Recently she narrated it at home, on the Sabbath, but on certain occasions she also narrates it on weekdays. She knows that Rabbi Ḥaim Pinto (Ḥaim Pinto the Elder) was buried in Mogador and that the commemorative celebrations in his honor are held after the Feast of the Tabernacles. Also, she points out that there is some connection between Rabbi Ḥaim Pinto and Rabbi David Ben-Barukh from Soos.[1]

Rabbi Ḥaim Pinto, who died in 1845, is indeed buried in Mogador, but the date of the festivities is the 26th of Ellul. In Moroccan folktales he is a mystic, a saint, and a miracle worker, and a collection of folktales relating to him and his family was published.[2] (The

---

[1] Rabbi David ben Barukh is a familiar Jewish-Moroccan holy character. Six folktales centering on him are preserved in IFA.

[2] Tarim, without date published in Casablanca. Another edition in two volumes was published in Israel. This, too, has no date.

Bags for Tefillin, phylacteries, twentieth century. By kind permission of the Israel Museum, Jerusalem.

book also contains tales of other saints.) As far as we know, his grandson, Ḥaim Pinto the Younger, who goes by this name to distinguish him from his grandfather, died in 1937 and was buried in Casablanca (some researchers are of the opinion that the painting in the *Shevah Ḥaim* is his portrait).[3] Of course, all this is not in agreement with the testimony of our tale.

---

[3] Cf. Ben-Ami 1976b, 153–220.

But it should be noted that the tale of the Pinto family narrated here recurs as a tale attributed to an anonymous rabbi.[4]

The genre to which the narrative belongs is the saints' legend, and the worldview that underlies it is numinous-miraculous. It teaches the values and behavioral norms governing the most critical moments of the life cycle. Incidentally, relating to the saints' legend as a "true story" that one "believes" is one feature of this genre. This is apparently the reason for, on the one hand, the anonymization of a specific, familial incident regarded as miraculous, and for a certain degree of family mythologization—utilizing the usual motifs of the saint's legend—of the narrator's family, on the other hand.

Observance of the Sabbath is one of the most important values of Judaism. The Sabbath differs from all the other Jewish holidays, which are basically of historic-religious orientation, inasmuch as its sanctity derives from mythic nature ritual, being a reenactment of the rest day observed by God. Hence the time of the Sabbath is of a quality that is as it were fulfilled in the great "mythic" time.[5]

Our narrative deals with the severest of tests: man must observe the Sabbath even if this involves the death of his child. The rabbi's strength is tried; he is required to sweep aside his sorrow and continue observing the Sabbath. We are reminded of the legend of Beruria, wife to Rabbi Meir, whose two sons died on the eve of the Sabbath: she did not share the shattering news with her husband lest he should sorrow over the death of his children and thus desecrate the Sabbath (Midrash Mishley 31).

Theodicy, which would be substantiated by the argument that children are nothing but pawns that God has temporarily left in the care of man, does not come in here because the child in this tale lives, as opposed to the child in the Beruria story, and God's verdict need not be vindicated.

Also, Beruria is of course exceptional: she is educated, daring, and broadminded. She is therefore not the typical Jewish mother figure, and this explains why the person exercising self-restraint in our tale, as well as in similar tales, is the father, not the mother. The father will not let his wife desecrate the Sabbath, and moreover, the wife does observe the Sabbath, not because the news of her child's death has been kept from her—which is what happens in the Midrashic tale—but because she defers to her husband, a rabbi and the descendant of a leading Jewish family.

---

[4] Cf. Noy 1964, no. 19 (IFA 3942).

[5] Cf. Eliade 1959, pp. 85–95.

Interestingly, the motif of child survival recurs in folktales deriving from the legend of Beruria and Rabbi Meir, the original Midrashic version of which does not, however, include this motif. A Moroccan parallel[6] is a case in point: an only son is born to an aging rabbi. The son dies in a landslide, but he is rescued and restored to life. The youth relates what happened to him in another world and how he was rescued by an old man (the Prophet Elijah) who removed the boulders that had piled up on top of his body.

However, in the version by Rabbi Nissim of Kiru'an, in *Hibur Yafe Me'hayeshuah*,[7] the news of the boys' death was false: in actual fact, a miracle happened, and the boys remained alive. Rabbenu Nissim therefore tends to tone down the supernatural, miraculous element, whilst in our version, as well as in parallel versions in the IFA, the change in the natural order of things is forcefully stated, and the boys' lives are restored.

Notice that the narrator of our tale attempts to raise the level of credibility and probability of the supernatural motifs by the inclusion of tangible, concrete details. This may be seen at the beginning and at the end of the tale: the events narrated happened to her own family, the Abu-Ḥazera family of Netivot (in Israel) is mentioned, and we learn that the boy whose life was saved did well for himself in Canada.

The full force of the trial in our version of the narrative is reflected in time: on the one hand the proliferation of actions performed by the couple slows down time and underlines the difficulties, while on the other hand a sense of deceleration highlights the fact that the couple are determined to observe all the commandments relating to the Sabbath, even on a day like this.

Questions as to the whereabouts of the child—which the Beruria tale assigns to Rabbi Meir—are asked by the wife's mother, as the husband and wife are both fully cognizant of the true state of affairs.

A concentrated restatement of the prohibition against mourning on the Sabbath is included in the Midrash Asseret Ha'dibrot:

> And God chose the Seventh Day for himself and He called it Hemdat Yamim (The Loveliest of Days), for on that day He joined heaven and earth, and He blessed it, as the Scriptures say 'And God blessed the Seventh Day and He sanctified it,' for on that day he rested and did no work, and he gave it to His Chosen People, the People of Israel, *so there should not be any sorrow*

---

[6] IFA 6626. Narrated by Abraham Attiya, recorded by Moshe Rabi.

[7] Edited by H. S. Hirschberg (Jerusalem, 1954), pp. 53–54.

*in their midst, for God gave it to us to rejoice in,*[8] and even those who languish in Hell must rest on the Sabbath Day. (Midrash of the Ten Commandments, The Fourth Commandment).

"He who observes the Sabbath is like a person who observes all the commandments of the Tora." (Yerushalmi, Nedarim, 83). Our tale supports these norms: it tells us that the highest reward goes to those who abstain from desecration of the Sabbath even at the most trying times in their lives. The principle of reciprocity applies: he who overcomes his sorrow in order to observe the Sabbath will be rewarded with joy; an added principle applies, that is, of crediting the merits of the fathers to the account of the children, in this case the merits of Rabbi Ḥaim Pinto.

The conclusion of the narrative with the narrator reverting to the merits of the family and anchoring the tale in present-day reality is a feature of the Jewish-Moroccan saints' legend.[9]

Incidentally, a similar folktale that centers on a father is in Midrash Va'Yikra Raba 20, 3. It involves a prominent personage in the city of Kabul whose son was getting married. When the guests were having dinner, the father told his son to go to the loft and get a cask. In the loft, the son was bitten by a snake, and he died. When his father followed him to the loft, he found his son dead, his body lying alongside some casks. When the guests had finished their meal, he said: "Gentlemen, you did not come here to bless the bridegroom. You came to bless his body. You did not come to walk my son to the wedding canopy. You came to lower him into his grave."

This tale, too, was presumably narrated in the framework of narratives told to comfort mourners. Following the precepts of normative Judaism, it suggests that the bereaved family should try to cope with misfortune and should exercise self-restraint. The father allows the wedding to proceed because a public festivity takes priority over the sorrow of a single individual. Moreover, by exercising self-restraint, the bereaved parent accepts God's judgment. Herein he resembles Beruria, who did not desecrate the Sabbath and accepted God's judgment.

We noted above that our narrative stresses the public duty of Sabbath observance; the underlying principle of theodicy is not clearly brought into focus.

---

[8] Italics added.

[9] An informant from Beth-She'an is a case in point: this man testified before me that his father studied Tora with the Prophet Elijah—a well-known motif of the folktale (H.B.I.).

# DAVID SERUYA

**DAVID SERUYA** was born in 1920. His parents were called Mass'ud and Esther. He was born in the town of Safru, Morocco, where he lived until he immigrated to Israel. His mother died following his birth, and he was raised by his grandmother, Rivka. His father was a very religious person who used to narrate religious tales to his family. David had eight years of Jewish education, and then he became a peddler wandering in the area between his town and the big city of Fez.

He and his wife Ḥasiba have seven children and twelve grandchildren. Although he came to Israel in 1956, the language spoken in his house is Judeo-Arabic. The stories he knows were narrated by the older people in his town and by people he met during his wanderings.

He loves narrating, and his son Asher recorded many of his narratives. These are deposited in the Israel Folktale Archives.

# If God Cares for Me, He Will Punch a Hole in the Ceiling and Pour Down Riches

FROM: DAVID SERUYA

There was a Jew who worked very hard to earn his bread. One of those days when he was loitering in the market he heard a Jew say: "If God wants to care for me, He will punch a hole in the ceiling and pour down riches." When he heard the sentence the Jew uttered, he stopped working, went back home, spread the carpet, and lay down to sleep all the time.

When his wife argued with him, saying: "Get up, go out and work," he would reply: "If God wants to give me something, he will make a hole in the ceiling and money will pour down."

When the woman realized there was no other way out, she left the house and started working. Every day she would chop down trees in the forest and sell the wood to housholds for heating and cooking. One day, as she was working away in the forest she saw a tree full of precious stones—pearls and diamonds. She decided not to take this treasure to her husband, but rather call her brothers so they could benefit from this divine treasure because her husband did not care what happened at home.

Her brothers went into the forest with mules and horses carrying many boxes and barrels for the precious stones and diamonds, when all of a sudden the tree filled up with snakes, scorpions, and other dangerous reptiles—instead of all the precious stones and diamonds. The brothers said angrily: "Don't you feel ashamed, sister? You have brought your brothers here so they should die of snakebite—is this the treasure you told us about?"

She replied: "And yet I ask you to pick all that is on the tree, take it to my house and throw it from the ceiling down onto my husband because he has not done any work for years, and all the hard work and raising the children is on my back."

The brothers collected all the snakes and went to town; their sister showed them her house and made them climb up onto the roof. The brothers made a hole in the ceiling and poured all they had in their sacks down into the room where the husband was sleep-

A candlestick and plate from Shlomi.

ing. Then they left the place in a hurry, after having stopped up the hole they had made in the ceiling.

The wife, who was sure her husband had died of snakebite, stepped into the room—and how surprised was she when she saw that all those snakes and reptiles had turned back into precious stones, diamonds and pearls, the way they had been on the tree. Her husband had not noticed anything and was sound asleep when his wife woke him, her face expressing surprise at all the light shining in her house. She asked him: "Where does all this wealth in our house come from?"

—"Of course," he replied: "I told you that if God wanted to give me riches, he would make a hole in the ceiling and pour down money." Of course, it never occurred to him that his wife had wanted to kill him, and God had upset her plan that all the treasure should be given to her brothers because her husband was lazy.

Then her husband got up, took one precious stone from among all the treasure, went to the market, and brought home a lot of money given to him in payment of the precious stone, and he built a new house, bought his sons all they needed, and became a very wealthy man.

## *Commentary:* IFA 16418

### IF GOD CARES FOR ME, HE WILL PUNCH A HOLE
### IN THE CEILING AND POUR DOWN RICHES

The narrative is a conglomerate of Aarne-Thompson 834 A: "The pot of gold and the pot of scorpions," with seven parallel versions in IFA,[1] and Aarne-Thompson 1645 B*: "God will care for all."[2]

The story's underlying worldview is fatalistic: God will provide for all needs of the true believer. Hence the protagonist stops working and goes to sleep, waiting for God's gifts.

To get the narrative message across, a confrontation between the sexes, between husband and wife, is employed. The husband represents the positive value of complete trust in God; he is the protagonist who is rewarded when the story draws to a close. Conversely, the wife is the antagonist who negates the values regarded as holy by the narrating society. She takes exception to her husband's views and insists that he should go out and get a job. When he refuses, she goes out and finds herself a job working in the forest. Thus she flouts the conventions of her society that require a woman to do her husband's bidding and obey him. More than that, she offends the moral laws of her society in that she leaves the house and stays in the forest alone, with no one to protect her. Again she flouts the conventions when she discovers a treasure and is loyal to her brothers, not her husband, whom she finally tries to kill. The woman does not only offend the dictates of her society, but she also disbelieves in God. She does not believe that God can care for her husband and supply him with money, and she even wishes to punish him for his faith when she tries to substitute for God and commands her brothers to go up to the roof and drop scorpions through the hole instead of the money her husband believes God will send him.

Interestingly, the wife is not punished for her misdeeds, and in this the narrative differs from other stories of this type. The principle of "as you treat others so shall they treat you" does not seem to apply to her, and she is not hurt by the reptiles that were meant to end her husband's life. Her punishment is failure: her scheme did not work, and she had to face the fact that she had made a mistake.

---

[1] Parallel versions are from Iraqi Kurdistan (5), Persian Kurdistan (1), Persia (1).

[2] Parallel version are from Morocco (1), Tunisia (1), Sefardi Israel (1), Israel Druze (1), Yemen (1), Turkish Kurdistan (2), Iraqi Kurdistan (3), Iraq (1), Persia (2), Afghanistan (1), Poland (1).

A cover for a Mezuzah, twentieth century. S. Papenhaim collection. By kind permission of the Israel Museum, Jerusalem.

Though the narrative is a sacred legend, it also contains a humoristic element, which is given expression by the husband's refusal to get up in the morning, and the wife's astonishment in the closing passage of the narrative.

# Juḥā Sells His House

FROM: DAVID SERUYA

Juḥā decided to sell his house, but before doing so he drove a nail into a wall right in the middle of the house. Whenever someone came to inquire, Juḥā said he was selling under one condition: except for the nail, everything was for sale. A certain Jew decided to buy the house, for a mere nail in the wall would not be an obstacle; they agreed on all the conditions in writing and signed.

When Juḥā received the money and left the house, he started walking about in the streets and whenever he found a cadaver he would hang it onto the nail in the house that he had previously owned. Several weeks passed, and Juḥā kept on doing the same thing day after day. The man who had bought the house could not complain because this was what they had agreed upon in the contract. But the stench and the dirt in the house got worse every day, until staying in that place became a nightmare. The buyer of the house collected his belongings and left the house and did not come back again.

And since then the folk term "Juḥā's nail" has become a household word.

## Commentary IFA 16415

### JUḤĀ SELLS HIS HOUSE

Typologically the narrative belongs to the group of jokes and anecdotes. Its number is Aarne-Thompson 1542*C: "Man sells house, but for a nail." IFA has several versions of this narrative type, all of which derive from the Muslim cultural area.[1]

Juḥā, the protagonist of the narrative, is a bit of a fool as well as a bit of a schemer, and he is a frequently occurring protagonist in Sefardi Jewish folktales, and generally of folktales told by Jews who lived in the cultural area of Islam. He is the counterpart of Hershele of Ostropol who was popular with East European Jews. Every culture needs a character who is both a fool and a schemer, and each ethnic group adapts this character to its own specific needs and concepts (Alexander 1980).

These tales are an expression of, and a lesson in, popular practical wisdom. They show how the weak survive in common everyday situations. The saying at the end of the narrative "and since then, the folk term 'Juḥā's nail' has become well known," which adds an etiological dimension to the tale, indicates that we are in fact dealing with popular practical wisdom, equally present in other genres, such as sayings and proverbs.

---

[1] The narratives are from Morocco (1), Libya (1), Arabs in Israel (1), Yemen (2), Persia (2).

# ASHER DAYAN

ASHER DAYAN was born in Marakesh (Morocco) in 1932. His father passed away when he was three years old, and he was raised by his mother Ḥaviva. From the first years he remembers his mother telling stories. He married his wife Saada in 1953, and in 1956 they immigrated to Israel and settled in Shlomi in 1962.

In Morocco Asher was educated at the Ḥeder of the organization "Otzar ha'Tora."[1] In Israel he attended a teachers' training college and taught at a school for about fifteen years. He currently runs the Shlomi post office.

Asher has eleven children, and he tells them some of his stories. He also tells stories to the family and to friends when they meet, especially in his synagogue where he is also a cantor.

---

[1] "Otzar ha'Tora" was a Jewish organization with a large educational network that started its activity in Morocco in 1948. Its aim was to teach Jewish traditional studies together with basic general studies. In 1960 "Otzar ha'Tora" had thirty-two schools in sixteen settlements. For in depth study of "Otzar ha'Tora," see Laskier 1981, 95.

# Rabbi Abraham Iben Ezra[1] is Sold into Slavery

### FROM: ASHER DAYAN

The story goes that once, when Rabbi Iben Ezra was traveling all over the world his luck was out, and he was shipwrecked. He was taken prisoner by pirates, who took him to the slave market and put him up for sale, along with all the others. As they were standing there people came and examined each of them, asking questions, trying to find out what each of them knew, and so on, when all of a sudden a priest walked by and spotted Iben Ezra. He saw that this was not an ordinary man, but someone special, and he asked him many questions, and he saw that this man was worth buying. He took him to his house, was mindful of his station, and was not hard on him, and gave him light work such as copying books and so on.

This priest was the chief priest in that country—and whenever the king invited people, he was the first to be asked. And on one occasion, when they were all assembled, they started talking about subjects such as contemplation and wisdom, and all the king's counselors tried to be clever; and the king noticed that the chief priest is trying to do better than all the others, humiliating them by preventing them from answering. The king thought carefully and said to him: "You see, your Highness the Pope, there are several questions that have been troubling me and to which I have been unable to find an answer. I would like to ask you, perhaps you can tell me the answer. If you tell me the answer, I will raise you to a higher rank, and if not—I am going to appoint another man to replace you, and you know what is going to happen next.

"The first question: We believe that God Almighty watches over the whole world. But tell me which side he turns his face to?!

"The second question: How much am I, the King, worth?

"The third question: What circles the world in twenty-four hours?"

The priest replied: "Give me a couple of days."

He looked in books and asked other priests, but to no avail. On

---

[1] See commentary.

the appointed day when he was due to appear before the king, he went to his scribe [the rabbi] and said: "Look here, I was mindful of your station, I respected you, I never made you work in the fields or do construction work. I have been asked three questions, these are the questions."

The rabbi replied: "I will go to the king for you. But I want you to give me your clothes, and if my answers are accepted—fine. If not, I will die instead of you."

The priest agreed. The rabbi went to the king's house. On his way there, he bought a beautiful cross. When he arrived, the king asked: "Are the answers ready?"

The rabbi replied: "Yes." The rabbi said: "The first question was: 'To which side does God Almighty turn His face?'" Then he asked for a candle to be lit, and he said to the king: "God inclines His face to where the flame turns."

Everybody stared at the flame. They all saw that it was steady and did not turn to any one side. The rabbi said: "As the flame gives light to everything and does not turn to any one side, so God watches over all the world."

Then the rabbi said: "The second question was: 'What is the king worth?' The answer is: "Your value equals precisely eight Francs." All those present were very angry: after all, the crown alone is covered with gold and jewels. The rabbi continued: "I bought this cross for ten Francs. What is the difference between the cross and the king? I did not want to say that the cross is worth eighty percent more than the king, so I said twenty percent, that is to say, he and his kingdom are worth less than the cross: eight Francs."

"The third question was: 'What is it that circles the world in twenty-four hours?' The answer is: the sun. The sun rises in the east and sets in the west. The next day it turns back east."

Next the king asked the rabbi: "What do I think about you?"

The rabbi replied: "I am sure you think this is not the priest, for the priest is unable to answer the questions. Now I want you to know who I am." He took off the hat and the robe, and lo and behold! the king saw a simple, poor Jew standing before him. He told him the whole story.

The King said: "What is it you want?"

Iben Ezra replied: "I do not want anything. I was born poor, and I am going to die poor. If you give me all you have, I am not going to use one cent. Whatever you want to give me I will divide into two parts—one half will go to poor Jews, and the other to the poor of your country."

A candleholder for a Ner Tamid in the synagogue, Morocco 1952. By kind permission of the Haifa Museum.

## *Commentary:* IFA 16385

### RABBI ABRAHAM IBEN EZRA IS SOLD INTO SLAVERY

The narrative belongs to Aarne-Thompson 922, "The shepherd substituting for the bishop answers the king's questions."[1] This is a Jewish version in which Rabbi Abraham Iben Ezra substitutes for a shepherd.[2] Rabbi Abraham Iben Ezra was born in Todela, Spain, in 1092 and the presumed date of his death is 1167. He was a poet, a Bible scholar, and a linguist. Until 1140 he was active in Kordoba. After 1160 he left Kordoba and was traveling in Italy, France, and England. This is reflected in the opening passage of the narrative. IFA has twenty narratives about Rabbi Abraham Iben Ezra. In this narrative in parallel with International Type Aarne-Thompson 922 I*b₂: "The emperor and the abbot," the protagonist who is requested

---

[1] Twenty-five versions of this narrative type are on file in the IFA. The narrators belonged to the following ethnic groups: Morocco (2), Greece (1), Arab Israel (2), Ashkenazi Israel (1), Yemen (1), Iraq (4), Persia (3), Bukhara (1), Afghanistan (3), Poland (1), Hungary (2), Russia (3), Eastern Europe (1).

For versions in print, see Noy 1979, no. 1; Cheichel 1970, no. 19; Nehmad 1966, no. 1.

[2] For Rabbi Abraham Iben Ezra in Jewish folktales, see Ben-Menahem 1943.

172

to answer questions is a bishop.[3] The first question and the image of the candle that serves in the answer to the question are common, especially in oicotype Aarne-Thompson 922*C: "Jews requested to answer questions or to perform tasks."[4] The question "How much is the king worth?" and the cross (Motif H 711.1) and the question "What is the king thinking about?" (Motif H 524.1—What am I thinking?) are typical features of the international narrative type.

The protagonist of this narrative, the one who answers the questions, is Rabbi Abraham Iben Ezra, distinct from the shepherd in the international version. There is a religious confrontation in addition to the confrontation between different social classes (shepherd and bishop in the international version, and servant and master in this narrative). The religious confrontation in this narrative, however, is not developed, and the superiority of Judaism derives from the fact that the rabbi is able to answer the questions whereas the priest fails to come up with a reply.

Actually the rabbi and the priest form a kind of alliance given expression by the rabbi's disguise into a priest and their joint effort to stand up to the king and answer his questions.[5]

Moreover, the end of our narrative suggests cooperation rather than confrontation, for the rabbi announces that he will give one-half of the money he is going to receive to poor Jews and the other half to poor gentiles. In an almost identical version from Morocco (IFA 10707), the tendency of turning the international type into a Jewish one, is reflected in the rabbi's view that the return to a Jewish home is better than wealth and honor in non-Jewish society.

---

[3] Thirty versions of this narrative type have been recorded by IFA, from Morocco, Tunisia, Egypt, Turkey, Sefardi Israel, Ashkenazi Israel, Arab Israel, Yemen, Iraq, Persia, Bukhara, Afghanistan, Georgia, Hungary, Russia. A comprehensive monograph on this narrative was written by Anderson (1923).

[4] Seventy-seven versions of this oicotype are on file in the IFA: Morocco (12), Tunisia (2), Libya (3), Egypt (4), Turkey (3), Syria (1), Lebanon (1), Sefardi Israel (5), Yemen (10), Persian Kurdistan (1), Iraq (12), Persia (2), Afghanistan (1), Romania (5), Czechoslovakia (1), Poland (10), Latvia (2), Russia (2). The following have appeared in print: Avitsuk 1965, no. 11; Noy 1964, nos. 49, 57, 62, 64; Cheichel 1970, no. 13; Noy 1967, no. 22; Baharav 1968, no. 65; Baharav 1964, no. 31; Noy 1963b, no. 88; Seri 1968, no. 7; Stahl 1976, no. 6; Noy 1963a, no. 38; Noy 1965, no. 33; Yeshiva 1963, no. 5.

[5] Dov Noy already referred to the appearance of Christian figures in Jewish Moroccan folktales. See Noy 1979, note to no. 1 (pp. 204–205).

# SULTANA SHOSHAN

SULTANA was born in 1905 in the town of Jedd, Morocco, where she worked as seamstress. In 1921 she married Mordekhai Shoshan. They have 12 children and 120 grandchildren and great-grandchildren. In 1951 she immigrated to Israel and settled in Shlomi, where she is still living. She likes to tell folk narratives and narratives about her family, especially about her brother who was killed in tragic circumstances.

# The Tailor's Son and the Magic Lantern

### FROM: SULTANA SHOSHAN

Once upon a time there was a tailor who had a wife and children, but no brothers and sisters and relatives.

Time went by and the tailor passed away. He was survived by his wife and children.

In that town there lived a star-gazer[1] who knew that a treasure was hidden there. This treasure could only be redeemed by the tailor's son.

The star-gazer went to the tailor's house and said he was the father's brother [the tailor's brother]. They replied: "But our father had no brother and no relatives."

The star-gazer replied: "Your father quarreled with me, and he did not like me, and that is why he severed connections with me, and I was longing to see you. Trust me." The star-gazer noticed that the house was empty and there was nothing in it, and he went out and bought dishes and rugs and food for them.

One day, the star-gazer said to the tailor's son: "Let's go on a trip to another town; we have not been out for a long time; come with me."

The tailor's son agreed; they left the house and bought meat and drink, and they took charcoal and equipment with them and left. The star-gazer led the tailor's son to a deserted place. The tailor's son was surprised, and he said: "Is this where you want to have a good time?"

The star-gazer replied: "Be patient, and keep walking until you come right into the middle of the desert."

The boy started thinking and said to himself: "This man wants to kill me."

When they reached a remote area where nobody could see them, the star-gazer sat down and lit a charcoal fire to burn incense till the earth opened up. Then the star-gazer said to the boy: "Climb

---

[1] In Hebrew "Ḥoze Ba'kokhavim."

down through this opening and collect all I tell you to collect and hand it to me."

The boy descended and found treasures of gold, silver, diamonds, and many valuables. He started collecting them, but when the star-gazer called in a loud voice, telling him to hand the treasure over to him, the ground above closed and the boy was inside. The star-gazer had run out of charcoal and incense, and that was why the opening in the ground closed.

The boy thought: "Now I am all alone. What am I going to do?" He started collecting the treasure that was lying close by. A handful of gold, and handful of silver, diamonds, emeralds, and so on. There was a lantern there. The boy reached out to grab it, when he heard a voice asking him what he wanted. He said: "Why did you leave me in here? I want to get out." And the lantern got him out. He collected all he had found and got out.

The lantern said: "Where would you like to go now?" He replied: "I want to go home."

The lantern replied: "Close your eyes and open them." When he opened his eyes he was at home.

His mother asked: "What happened to you?" He said the star-gazer had tried to kill him, and he told her all that had happened. He put all the treasure inside the house.

From that time onward he would address the lantern, saying: "Lantern, do your work." Then everything would be ready, lots of food, a house full of good things to eat and whatever you want.

One day the tailor's son said to his mother: "Mother, I want you to arrange my marriage. I want to marry the King's daughter."

His mother was surprised. She said: "How can a poor, simple woman like me ask for the hand of the king's daughter in marriage?" But her son insisted: he wanted to marry none but the king's daughter.

When she realized that her son had made up his mind, she agreed. He filled a large reed basket with gold, silver, precious stones and emeralds, diamonds and other valuables, and handed it to his mother, telling her to go to the king's house.

When she reached the gate of the palace, they stopped her. She was not strong enough to get in. The guards saw how she kept waiting for a long time, and they said: "She may be a poor woman who needs help. We will let her in and find out what it is she wants."

When she was brought before the king, she opened her basket and said: "My son wants to marry the king's daughter."

The king replied: "But where did you get all this treasure from? All there is in the palace is not worth as much as what you have in that basket. Very well, I agree: he may marry my daughter, but he must do everything I tell him." The mother said she wanted to speak to her son. The king agreed.

The king wanted the tailor's son to build a house of gold and emeralds for his daughter. The tailor's son said, "I agree."

The tailor's son went to the lantern, and when he said with his eyes closed: "Lantern, do your work," there rose the house all of gold and precious stones. The tailor's son left two windows unfinished, and then he went to the king and said: "Oh King, I want you to help me finish these two windows." The king panicked. He said: "How can I raise all the treasure to have the two windows finished?" He took counsel and tried to find a solution, but [he] was unable to raise money to have the two windows completed.

So the tailor's son came and had the windows done. Since there was no choice, the king gave his daughter in marriage to the tailor's son. After the wedding, the poor man's son asked his wife and the servants to take good care of the little lantern.

One day, the tailor's son went hunting. And the self-same stargazer came to town and started offering new, well-made lanterns for sale. He walked about crying in a loud voice: "Ladies who have old lanterns may exchange them for new ones."

He walked through the whole of the town until he reached the house of the tailor's son. The servant heard him and rushed to her mistress, telling her: "We have this old lantern in the house. Let's exchange it for a new one."

The king's daughter agreed and ordered the servant to call the peddler. The moment the peddler saw the lantern he became so very excited that he gave the king's daughter all the lanterns he had. Then he took the old lantern and went off.

The tailor's son returned home after the hunt, and lo and behold! the palace he built was no longer there, and his wife had disappeared too. He saddled his horse, and slaughtered cattle and sheep. These he took to the forest. He left the meat in the forest and disappeared.

All the animals of the forest came and ate their fill. One of the animals said: "We have had a regal meal, and we do not know who prepared it. Let's find out who did it, and let's reciprocate."

The tailor's son appeared and said: "It was me. I did it."

They asked him: "What do you want?"

He replied: "I want you to show me where the 'black slave' is."

The animals recoiled, saying: "That is very hard." But the tailor's son pleaded with them, asking them to show him the place. The animals agreed. For seven days and seven nights they led him along dangerous roads until finally they reached the town where the "black slave" lives. The tailor's son became a baker in that town.

In the meanwhile, the king's daughter refused to marry that man, the one who took her away. He punished her, that black slave, he gave her nothing but rye bread to eat and water to drink.

One day, the baker, the tailor's son stepped into the bakery and noticed an unusual loaf of bread among all the loaves of rye bread. The tailor's son asked what it meant, and one of the servant girls replied: "Our master brought the king's daughter from some town, and he wants to marry her, but she refuses. So he punishes her, putting her on rye bread and water so she should give in and marry him."

The tailor's son took the gold ring he was wearing on his finger and put it into the loaf. When the king's daughter received her daily loaf, she found the ring in it and she recognized it: it belonged to her husband. She started thinking how could she get in touch with him. She called a servant-girl and said: "Speak to the baker and tell him I do not want to marry that man, and now that you have given me a token tell me what to do."

The servant-girl did so.

The tailor's son said to the servant-girl: "Tell your mistress she should go to her master and agree to marry him. She should say: 'I give in. I am ready to marry you. Let us prepare a party and let's get married.' And when your master gets drunk, take a small flask of poison and pour it into his drink. In this way he will meet his end."

The king's daughter did so: she went to the "black slave" (her master) and agreed to marry him. He immediately commanded his servants to prepare the feast.

When it was time for the feast to begin the king's daughter said she wanted to be alone with her husband. He agreed. The king's daughter sat next to her husband ["the black slave"] enjoying the party till she noticed that her husband started getting drunk. She prepared the flask and poured the poison into his glass. The black slave started drinking, and his soul started leaving his body. The tailor's son came to the feast and spoke to the black slave: "So this is how you scheme and how you have a party?!"

The black slave begged for mercy, but the tailor's son cut off his head, took his wife and his lantern, and returned to his town.

Suddenly the king noticed that his daughter's palace, which had disappeared, was there again. He was very surprised, and he asked for an explanation. The tailor's son replied: "My power lies in this," and he showed him the lantern. Then he added: "It was your daughter who brought on all this trouble."

A traditional woman's dress in Tefilelat, Morocco. By kind permission of the Haifa Museum.

And from that day onward the tailor's son and the king's daughter lived together happily, and they took good care of their valuable possession.

## *Commentary:* IFA 16393

### THE TAILOR'S SON AND THE MAGIC LANTERN

This is a version of narrative type Aarne-Thompson 561: "Aladdin." In the IFA eight versions of the narrative type are deposited, all of which were recorded from Jewish narrators from Islamic countries.[1]

The story of Aladdin and the magic lantern is one of the most widely known classical fairy tales, owing to its many adaptations in writing. This version has a number of special characteristics. In most versions realistic characters appear who function both realistically and supernaturally, given a magic object. Likewise, supernatural characters appear in the tale, which are demons residing in the lantern and sometimes in the ring. In this narrative the realistic characters also function supernaturally. There is, for instance, the star-gazer who is called "the black slave" in the second part of the narrative, which suggests his involvement with black magic. With him, the supernatural function is expressed by knowledge of hidden and faraway things, by his ability to open a secret underground passage leading to hidden treasures, and finally by his ability to move the palace to his country thanks to the magic lantern he owns.

The tailor's son is also capable of functioning supernaturally as soon as he wins the right to the lantern. His supernatural function is expressed by the space jump he takes—straight from the underground to the surface and his house, and by the instant erection of the palace built from precious stones and precious metals, and finally by the removal of the palace to its original site.

As distinct from most versions, there are no supernatural characters here. The lantern, not the demons residing in it, performs all the functions: it speaks and causes the magic transformation. Therefore the magic object has the narrative role of the magical helpmate (Propp 1968), not another character.

The narrative has a number of spatial realms, one of which is the realm of the protagonist. The characterizations of this realm are few and functional for the narrative plot. The spatial objects men-

---

[1] Morocco (2), Tunisia (1), Egypt (1), Lebanon (1), Yemen (1), Persia (2). Two versions were printed: Noy 1966, no. 16; Avitsuk 1965, no. 35.

tioned are the house of the protagonist, the king's palace, where the mother is sent to negotiate her son's marriage, and the palace that the tailor's son builds at the king's bidding, assisted by the magic lantern.

The other spatial realm is the domain of the "black slave." This area to which he removes the palace and its contents is characterized by its remote location faraway from the spatial realm of the protagonist.

Two additional spatial realms are intermediate. First, the lonely desert serves as a transit space to be crossed in order to reach the underground world of treasures, and second, the forest, the kingdom of the animals, transfers the protagonist to the space of the "black slave."

This episode (animals render assistance) occurs only in this version. It contains elements of the animal fairy tale in which grateful animals return the favor the protagonist has done them (he has given them food). Also, the ability of the protagonist to converse with the animals without the use of the magic object is characteristic of the animal fairy tale, which takes communication between the world of man and the world of animals for granted. The spatial scheme is:

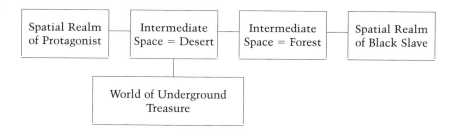

In the narrative, time is also endowed with characteristics of supernatural time. This is expressed by the space jump—vast distance is covered in a very short period of time. To demonstrate the relativity of the two times the narrator uses the image of shutting and opening eyes, an operation that takes very little time according to the concepts of real time, he allows the protagonist to take a short-cut, according to the concepts of supernatural time.

The story is a magic fairy tale, but it contains motifs of subtlety and deceit, characteristics of the realistic novella. To gain access to magic, the protagonists resort to subtlety. In dealing with their enemies they proceed with cunning, and they use clever stratagems to defeat them. This applies to the star-gazer who poses as the protagonists' uncle at the beginning of the story and to the tailor's son who poses as a baker, sends his wife the ring in a loaf of bread, and then instructs her how to deceive the black slave.

# YA'ACOV EDRI

YA'ACOV was born in 1929 in Emizmez in the Atlas mountains of Morocco. He is the son of Solomon and Ḥannah Edri. In Morocco he was a manager of a textile workshop. In 1956 he immigrated to Israel and settled in Shlomi. In the years 1964–1987 he was the secretary of the federation of workers in Shlomi. Ya'acov has nine children and eleven grandchildren.

In his childhood Ya'acov would listen to the folk narratives told by his parents. He still narrates to his children and his grandchildren.

# The Purim Miracle

### FROM: YA'ACOV EDRI

Before every holiday it was the custom for children in Morocco to sit in the Ḥeder[1] from early morning till evening and to study the rules and customs to be observed on that particular holiday. It is important for you to know this so you can understand the story I am going to tell you.

Everybody knows that kings in other countries had Jewish advisers; every king had a Jewish counsellor. And everybody knows, too, that the rabbis were loyal to the kings. When a king consulted with a rabbi and let him in on a secret, the rabbi would not betray him. Or again, if a rabbi heard something he would tell the king about it and bring the matter to his knowledge.

Once the king's minister noticed that the king consulted only with the rabbi and not with him. He came before the king, and he said to him: "Are you aware that the Jews are learning how to shoot and how to use firearms and how to fight you?"

The king replied: "How is that possible? The Jews are loyal to me, and I grant them more privileges than I allow the Arabs—and now they want to use firearms against me?"

He replied: "Yes."

The king said: "I do not believe it."

His deputy replied: "Come and see for yourself." He took the king [to the synagogue] on the eve of the Feast of Purim when they were reciting the Scroll of Esther. When the words "Arur Haman"[2] were pronounced, all the children started shooting their revolvers.

The king heard the shots, which were fired at regular intervals to underscore the words "Arur Haman," and he said: "You are right."

On the following day, the king sent for the rabbi, and he said to him: "I cannot understand why you should train your people in the use of firearms against me the moment you are granted equal rights."

The rabbi replied: "What did you hear?"

---

[1] A place where children are taught, literally "a room" (Ḥeder).

[2] In Hebrew, a curse upon Haman.

He replied: "I heard shots yesterday."

The rabbi said: "Please believe me! We have a story about Haman and Mordekhai. Haman wanted to destroy Mordekhai and his people, but in the end they hanged Haman. And from that time we observe a holiday to commemorate this event, and we recite the words "Arur Haman." When the congregation [in the synagogue] hears these words, they all start shooting.

The king sent for his minister, and he said to him: "So this is the story."

The deputy said to him: "That is not true. If it is true, let them bring this Mordekhai before you so he can tell you his story."

The rabbi did not know what to do. He declared a three-day public fast, telling the Jews to pray for the cancellation of this punishment.

All the Jews fasted for three days. And there was one man who did not observe the fast. He walked about in the streets and he ate. Another Jew said to this man: "Haven't you heard about the fast and about the king's threat? If we fail to bring Mordekhai before the king, we are all going to die."

The man answered: "Don't you worry. Eat and drink!"

The other Jew said: "How can we not worry? Hasn't the rabbi himself ordered us [to fast and pray]?" The Jew decided to bring this man before the rabbi, and he suggested that the rabbi should bring him before the king.

Every king has two guards who stand at the gate and then another man to protect him. The rabbi and the man went to the king's palace. When the guards saw the rabbi, they asked: "Where is Mordekhai?"

The man whom the rabbi was taking to the king's palace said: "I will knock the guards over." He knocked over the first two guards, and the third guard fled and said to the king: "This Mordekhai has arrived, and he has already killed two men. What are we to do?"

The king said: "Speak to him in a quiet voice."

The rabbi came before the king, and the king's minister is there next to him.

The minister said: "Are you Mordekhai?"

The man replied: "Yes. I hanged Haman on a tall tree."

The minister said: "If that is so, show us something to prove you are Mordekhai."

The man replied: "Your Majesty, do you have a long knife?"

The king said: "Yes."

The man asked for a table, too.

He said to the king: "Order your minister to stand on this table

An amulet, Hamsa, Morocco. By kind permission of the Haifa Museum.

so I can show you how I hack him to pieces within a minute, and how I place my hands on him and put him together again."

The king said: "All right."

The minister who is standing next to him says: "No, Sir, you need not do that. I believe you. Now I believe you."

## *Commentary:* IFA 16421

### THE PURIM MIRACLE

We are dealing with Jewish oicotype Aarne-Thompson 922*C (IFA): "Jews requested to answer questions or to perform tasks." Seventy-seven parallel narratives in the IFA were recorded from narrators of several different Jewish ethnic groups.[1] Although the narrator names the narrative "The Purim Miracle" it contains no supernatural events, and it does therefore not belong to the genre of the sacred legend, which the title seems to suggest. As the issue raised in the narrative is solved by means of a ruse, we are dealing with a novella of subtlety and deceit.

The narrative treats a theme that frequently recurs in folktales told by the Jews of the Diaspora: the confrontation between Jews and gentiles, one of the main problems that faced the narrating society.

---

[1] Cf. p. 173, note 4.

The temporal setting of the story is the feast of Purim, and its structure is that of the Book of Esther which is recited in the synagogue on the day of the feast. The tale of Esther is laid in the Diaspora, in Persia, and the protagonists are placed at the three corners of a triangle. At the positive pole there are Mordekhai and Esther, and at the negative pole there is Haman. The neutral protagonist is Ahasverus, who "reigned from India even unto Ethiopia, over a hundred and seven and twenty provinces." Ahasverus is courted by both the protagonists at the positive pole and the antagonist Haman; both try to win him over. In the Book of Esther, Haman envies Mordekhai and tries to destroy him and his people. In our narrative the non-Jewish adviser (located at the negative pole) envies the rabbi (who is located at the positive pole together with the anonymous Jew) and brings false charges against him and his people.

The narrator goes to great lengths to underline the fact that the Jews were loyal to their king, a stance considered important by the narrating society that had often been looked upon with suspicion.

In the Book of Esther and in this narrative the two counsellors each try to win the king's support, and at the end it looks as though the non-Jew is gaining the upper hand. The king's lack of familiarity with the customs of the Jews, who make a lot of noise whenever Haman's name is mentioned during the service, as well as the insistence of the vengeful counsellor tip the scale against the Jews who are told to bring Mordekhai the Jew, the protagonist of the Book of Esther, before the king to substantiate their story.

The day of fast and penitence that the Jews subsequently observe averts the danger and invokes God's help. However, this narrative is not a sacred legend, and there is no divine intervention. On this count, too, the influence of the Book of Esther is evident. In the Book of Esther the Jews are saved thanks to the resourcefulness and cunning of human beings (Mordekhai and Esther). In this narrative matters proceed on the same level. Because the counsellor wants the Jew to prove that he is indeed Mordekhai, the Jew accedes to his request and proposes that he will perform a miracle: he will cut the counsellor to pieces and reassemble the pieces at one blow. As a result of this strategy the counsellor, who fears for his life, is ready to admit his error and to justify the claim of the Jew. Narratives of this type indicate that the narrating society views resourcefulness, subtlety, and cunning in addition to normative religious acts such as fasting and prayer as necessary to survive in a hostile world.

# Eliyahu Abu-Ḥatzera

ELIYAHU ABU-ḤATZERA was born in Ozurath, Morocco, in 1926. He was married when he was nineteen years old and has ten children. In Morocco Eliyahu was a shoemaker. He immigrated to Israel in 1956. At first he lived in the village of Gefen, and then he moved to Shlomi. He worked as a superintendent in a youth club, and whenever one of the instructors was missing Eliyahu took his place by narrating folktales to the group. Most of his stories he heard from his father when he was young. In 1990 Eliyahu had a stroke; he is paralyzed and hospitalized.

# *Nobody Can Escape His Fate*

### FROM: ELIYAHU ABU-ḤATZERA

There were two brothers, one was rich and the other was poor. The poor brother had ten children and a pregnant wife. In those days people had no candles, and of course there was no electricity.

One night the rich brother dreamt that his brother's wife would have a boy, and this boy would be his heir and inherit all his money. In the meanwhile, the poor man's wife went into labor, and there was no light in the house. The woman said to her husband: "Go to your brother's place and bring us some oil so we can have some light." He went there, and he asked his brother for a little oil, explaining that his wife had gone into labor. But the rich brother chased him away and didn't give him a thing. The poor brother returned home weeping, and his tears dropped into a dish, and it was filled to the brim. He told his wife what had happened. His wife told him to dip the wick into the dish full of tears, and God is all powerful. The poor man did so, he lit the wick, dipping it into the dish full of tears, and there was light till she had the baby.

The child grew and was six years old. The rich brother came to the poor brother's house and said: "Look here, you have ten children, and I have nothing, let me have this boy, I will raise him, I will teach him, and I will take good care of him."

At once, the poor brother gave him the boy. (When the poor brother had asked for some oil he got nothing, but when the rich brother wanted the child, his wish was instantly met.)

When the rich uncle had kept the boy at his place for a week, he took him to a shepherd. He said to the shepherd: "Take the boy to a cave and kill him. Dip his shirt in his blood, and bring me the shirt."

The shepherd took the child with him. His intention was to kill him. When he raised his arm to strike him down, the boy laughed. At that moment the shepherd was filled with compassion for him, and he decided he would not kill him. He said to himself: "Here I am, preparing to kill him, and he laughs." The shepherd took a sheep and slaughtered it; then he took the boy's shirt, dipped it in the sheep's blood and took it to the rich man. The rich man hid the shirt.

The boy remained inside the cave.

The rabbi in that town had two cows, and he used to prepare milk and butter. On the following day, the two cows were pastured by a student of the rabbi's. One of the cows strayed into the cave in which the boy was staying. The child started suckling the cow's milk. [Milk contains vitamins[1] and many other things, God sent the child this cow so he could survive.] The following day the cows were again pastured, and again one of the cows walked into the cave, and the boy suckled all its milk to the last drop. When the rabbi's student returned the cows to the cowshed, the rabbi's wife started milking them. And lo! and behold: the udder of one cow is full, and the udder of the other is empty. The woman spoke to the rabbi, her husband. She said: "Look, these two cows were pastured by the student, and there! one is full of milk, and the other is completely empty."

The rabbi replied: "Maybe the student was hungry or thirsty, and so he drank some of the milk. Tomorrow I am going to pasture the cows together with the student, and we'll see what happens."

The next day, they left the house to pasture the cows, they came to an open space, and the rabbi and the student sat down and studied the Tora, and they took no notice of the cows. Again, one of the cows strayed into the cave, and again the child drank its milk to the last drop. When the cow emerged from the cave, the rabbi saw it, and he noticed there was, again, a difference between the two cows.

When they came back home, his wife was surprised. She said: "Again, one cow is full, and the other is empty."

The rabbi answered: "As a matter of fact, we went into the fields in order to find out how, precisely, this has come about. But when we reached the open spaces, we studied, and we did not pay attention to what, precisely, was going on. Tomorrow I'll go out by myself and find out what happens."

The next day, the rabbi left the house and drove the cows to pasture. He followed them wherever they went. Again, one of the cows steps into the cave, and the rabbi follows it. The rabbi saw the child suckling the cow's milk. The rabbi saw that this was a Jewish child [the boy was circumcised]. He took off his coat and wrapped the boy in the coat. He brought him home. The rabbi said to his wife: "This is a child whose parents are Jewish, and he drinks the cow's milk." The rabbi's wife took the child, washed him and dressed him, and took care of him.

In the meanwhile, the rich man's wife became pregnant and had a girl.

---

[1] Probably an Israeli influence.

The boy spent eighteen years in the rabbi's house. They taught him well, and he became a very learned man.

The eighteen-year-old boy said to the rabbi: "You see, I have been studying for eighteen years. I would like to get out and look around for a little while."

The rabbi replied: "Please do."

The boy did a bit of traveling, and he met a man. The man said to him: "I want you to know that you are the son of a cow."

The boy was surprised. He said: "What do you mean—I have no father and no mother? I am just the son of a cow?" He returned to the rabbi's house. He said to him: "Are you my father, and is that my mother?"

The rabbi said: "No." And he told him how he had found him.

The boy thanked the rabbi very much—for he had clothed him, had given him food and drink, and had taught him. He walked for some distance until he met his cousin. He asked her: "Where is there a synagogue?"

His cousin took him to the synagogue, and then she spoke to her father. She said: "Father, a young man came, and he asked me where the synagogue was. Now I want to marry this young man. If I don't, I am going to take my own life."

The father said: "We can't force matters. I will go to the synagogue, and I will invite him to our house, and I will talk to him." The uncle went to the synagogue and lectured; after the lecture he spoke to the young man and invited him. The young man accepted the invitation.

The uncle said: "My daughter took you to the synagogue, and when she came back she said she wanted to marry you, or else she would take her own life. Now, if you are prepared to marry her, I will leave you all my inheritance, for she is my only daughter." (His dream was beginning to materialize).

The young man agreed, and then he asked: "Is there a rabbi here?"

His uncle said: "There is."

They went there, prepared the marriage certificate, and made over the inheritance to the young man. They performed the wedding ceremony, and he married his cousin.

One evening, all the family sat down to have a meal together. And the uncle—he held his head in his hands. His son-in-law asked him: "What are you doing that for? We do not lack anything—we have all we want."

He said: "I have just remembered a wrong I committed."

He said to him: "What is it you did?"

191

He said to him: "My brother has ten children and he is poor, and I was rich and I had no children. His wife was pregnant, and he asked me to give him a little oil, and I chased him away and gave him nothing. And then he had a son, and I dreamt that this son would inherit my property. When the son was six years old I went to see my brother, and I asked him to give me his son. I told him I would raise him and give him an education and he instantly gave me the boy. And as I had that dream, I asked a shepherd to take the boy to a cave, to slaughter him, to dip his shirt in his blood and bring me the shirt."

The son-in-law asked: "Where is the shirt?"

The uncle replied: "Right here," and he produced it.

The son-in-law asked: "And who is your brother?"

He said: "Right here."

The following day, the Bible scholar said to his wife: "Send for your uncle. I want him to come here."

The uncle came. The Bible scholar asked: "Did you give your brother a child of yours?"

He answered: "Yes."

The Bible scholar said: "And did he live in his house for a week and two, and were you then told he had disappeared?"

He replied: "Yes."

The Bible scholar said to him: "Listen! I dreamt that your son is alive."

The poor uncle was very happy; he embraced the Bible scholar and kissed him. The Bible scholar took a golden nugget and a bag full of silver, and he said to him: "Take that, and see to it that your home and family want nothing, and I will bring you the child."

The poor man took the money and went home. He said to his wife: "God sent us an angel from Heaven."

She asked: "Why?"

He said to her: "The young man who married my niece dreamt that our son is still alive. He promised to bring him here. He gave me a golden nugget and a bag full of silver and sent me home."

The mother was very happy, and she went to see the Bible scholar. She embraced him, and she kissed him. Then she asked: "Is our son really alive?"

He replied: "Yes. I will bring him here either on Monday or on Thursday."

The mother left.

The Bible scholar said to his wife: "Send for the shepherd." The Bible scholar said to the shepherd: "Come with me. We are going to the king's palace."

The shepherd was surprised: "What have I done?"

He answered: "You come with me."

When they came to the king's palace the Bible scholar said to the king: "I want you to record that the house in which the shepherd lives is his own, as of now, it belongs to him; and all the sheep he pastures are his, too." He also gave him a bag full of money.

Now the Bible scholar went to see the poor man's wife. He told her: "Take your children, line them up in a row and sit down on one side, and tell your husband to sit on the other side. I will bring the child here—as early as Monday."

On Monday the woman lined up the children the way she had been told, and the Bible scholar arrived. He said to the poor man: "Is it true that you went to your brother's house and asked for a little oil when your wife was pregnant? And is it true that he chased you away?"

He replied: "Yes."

Then he asked: "When the boy was five or six years old, did you give him to your brother, and did your brother tell you after a week or two that the boy had disappeared?"

He replied: "Yes."

The Bible scholar said: "I want you to know that your brother handed the boy over to a shepherd, telling him to slaughter him in a cave, dip his shirt in his blood and bring him the shirt. And the shepherd did not do so, and the boy's life was spared and he remained in the cave, and a cow came and he drank its milk, and this cow belonged to the rabbi, and the rabbi came and tried to find out who was drinking the milk, and he found a boy. The rabbi took the child home and raised him and taught him till the age of eighteen. When the boy was eighteen, he said he would like to do a bit of traveling, and as he was traveling he met a man who said to him: 'I want you to know that you are the son of a cow.' Then he went to the rabbi and enquired who his parents were. And the rabbi told him all that had happened starting from the moment he found him in the cave."

When he had finished the story, the woman asked: "You promised you would bring our son. Where is he?"

The Bible scholar replied: "I am your son."

A Jewish-Moroccan bride dress. By kind permission of the Haifa Museum.

## *Commentary:* IFA 16383

### NOBODY CAN ESCAPE HIS FATE

The narrative belongs to type Aarne-Thompson 930: "The prophecy." We are told about the future greatness of the boy, which leads to attempts to destroy him. Twenty-eight versions of this narrative type are on file in the IFA.[1]

Our narrative opens with a confrontation against an economic familial background. A rich brother dreams that his poor brother's son will inherit his fortune: hence he turns him away when he asks for some oil to light a lamp as his wife is going into labor.

Here the narrator uses the familiar motif from Talmudic literature, that is, the story of Rabbi Hanina Ben Dossa and his daughter: "Once Rabbi Hanina Ben Dossa noticed that his daughter was sad. It was the eve of the Sabbath, and it was getting dark. He said to her: 'My daughter, why are you sad?' She said: 'I mistook a bottle of vinegar for a bottle of oil, and I used the vinegar to light the lamp for the Sabbath.' He said to her: 'My daughter, what do you care? He who told the oil to burn will tell the vinegar to burn.' The vinegar burned until they used the flame to light the candle for the ceremony of Havdala" (Ta'anit 25).

In our narrative there is no dishful of vinegar, but rather a dishful of poor men's tears, and it is the woman who says: "Dip the wick into the dishful of tears and light it, and God is all-powerful." The poor man did so: he dipped the wick into the dishful of tears and lit it, and there was light until the woman had given birth.

Again, the rich brother tries to lure the child on to destruction. He tricks his brother into handing the boy over to him and tells a shepherd to slaughter him. The shepherd does not do the rich man's bidding because the child laughs as he is getting ready to strike. Laughter to meet a homicidal situation is a frequent motif in folk narratives (Motif S 261.1). The boy's life is spared; he is abandoned (Motif S 301) and finally saved (Motif R 131) and raised far from his home (Motif S 354).

---

[1] The versions are from Morocco (3), Tunisia (4), Algeria (1), Turkey (1), Syria (1), Sefardi Israel (2), Ashkenazi Israel (2), Yemen (4), Iraqi Kurdistan (1), Persian Kurdistan (1), Iraq (5), Persia (2), Afghanistan (2), Poland (1), Eastern Europe (areas unspecified) (1). For printed versions, see Noy 1966, nos. 54, 66; Noy 1971, no. 2; Noy 1963, no. 97; Noy 1963a, no. 49; Noy 1965, nos. 5, 80; Kagan 1964, no. 4; Marcus 1966, no. 12; Mizrahi 1967, no. 30.

In the manner of tales of fate, the decree of fate comes true as the story reaches its close. In our narrative this is accomplished by means of a meeting with a cousin whom the boy eventually marries.[2] The narrator describes the parent-son encounter at great length, and the searching questions put to the son are a special feature of this version in which encounters and questions close the information gap of all the protagonists. Other versions emphasize the punishment of the antagonist. In our narrative the cruel uncle is not singled out for physical punishment; his punishments are a guilty conscience and the realization that his schemes are foiled and the prophecy comes true.

---

[2] This is connected with the motif "A Marriage Decreed by the Divine Will." For an exhaustive treatment, see Shenhar 1982, 134–145.

# Bibliography

Aarne, A., and S. Thompson. 1961. *The Types of the Folktale: A Classification and Bibliography.* 2d rev. (Folklore Fellow Communications 184). Helsinki: Suomalainen Tiedeakatemia.

Alexander, T. 1981. "The Character and the Town—Judeo-Spanish humoristic tales." *Pe'amim* 7:64–82.

Alexander, T., and D. Noy. 1989. *The Treasure of Our Father.* Jerusalem: Misgav Yerushalaim.

Aminof, I. 1974. *The Emir and the Jewish Widow.* Haifa: Israel Folktale Archives Publications Series.

Anderson, W. 1923 *Kaiser und Abt: Die Geschichte eines Schwanks.* (Folklore Fellow Communications 42). Helsinki: Suomalainen Tiedeakatemia.

Attias, M. 1976. *The Golden Feather.* Haifa: Israel Folktale Archives Publications Series.

Avitsuk, J. 1965. *The Tree that Absorbed Tears.* Haifa: Israel Folktale Archives Publications Series.

Baharav, Z. 1964 *Sixty Folktales Collected from Narrators in Ashkelon.* Haifa: Israel Folktale Archives Publications Series.

———. 1968. *From Generation to Generation.* Tel-Aviv: Ya'ad.

Bar-Itzhak, H. 1987. "Saints' Legends As Genre in Jewish Oral Tradition." Ph.D. Diss., Jerusalem: The Hebrew University.

———. 1992. "'Smeda Rmeda who destroys her luck with her own hands'— a multi-disciplinary study of the Cinderella story of Moroccan Jews." *Jerusalem Studies in Jewish Folklore* 13:323–348.

Ben-Ami, I. 1976a. "The Presence of Demons in the Moroccan Jewish Home." In *The Jews of Morocco—Studies in Their Culture.* Jerusalem: Reuben Mas.

———. 1976b. "Shevah Haim." In *The Jews of Morocco—Studies in Their Culture.* Jerusalem: Reuben Mas. Pp. 153–220.

Ben-Amos, D. 1969. "Analytical Categories and Ethnic Genres." *Genre* 2:275–301.

# BIBLIOGRAPHY

————. 1975. *Sweet Words, Storytelling Events in Benin.* Philadelphia: Institute for the Study of Human Issues.

Ben-Menahem, N. 1943. *Abraham Iben Ezra, Conversations and Folk Legends.* Jerusalem: Igud Sofrim Dati'im.

Ben-Yehezkel, M. 1965. *Ma'assioth Book.* Tel-Aviv: Dvir.

Bettelheim, B. 1977. *The Uses of Enchantment, The Meaning and Importance of Fairy-tales.* New York: Vintage Books.

Buber, S. ed. [1885] 1946. *Midrash Tanhuma.* Vilna: Rom.

Cheichel, E. 1970. *A Tale for Each Month 1968–1969.* Haifa: Israel Folktale Archives Publications Series.

————. 1973. *A Tale for Each Month 1972.* Haifa: Israel Folktale Archives Publications Series.

Cox, M. P. 1893. *Cinderella.* London: David Nutt.

Dawkins, R. M. 1953. *Modern Greek Folktales.* Oxford: Clarendon Press.

Dundes, A. 1991. *The Blood Libel Legend, A Casebook in Anti-Semitic Folklore.* Madison: University of Wisconsin Press.

Eberhard, W. and P. N. Boratav. 1953. *Typen tuerkischer Volksmaerchen.* Wiesbaden: F. Steiner.

Eliade, M. 1959. *The Sacred and the Profane.* New York: Harper and Row.

Fallah, S. and A. Shenhar. 1978. *Druze Folktales.* Jerusalem: Israel Folktale Archives Publications Series.

Gaster, M. [1924] 1968. *The Exempla Of The Rabbis.* Leipzig-London: Asia Publishing Co.

————. 1934. *Ma'asseh Book: Book of Jewish Tales and Legends Translated from the Jewdeo-German.* 2 vols. Philadelphia: The Jewish Publication Society of America.

Ginzberg, L. 1966–1975. *The Legends of The Jews.* Ramat-Gan: Massada. (Hebrew version).

Haviv, Y. 1966. *Never Despair.* Haifa: Israel Folktale Archives Publications Series.

Hasan-Rokem, G. 1982. "The Research of the Processes of Change in the Folk Narrative." *Jerusalem Studies in Jewish Folklore* 3:129–137.

Jason, H. 1971. "Formalism and the Study of Folk Literature." *Hasifrut* 3, 1:53–84.

Kagan, Z. 1964. *A Tale for Each Month 1963.* Haifa: Israel Folktale Archives Publications Series.

Katzir, Y. 1982. "Preservation of Jewish Ethnic Identity in Yemen: Segregation and Integration as Boundary Maintenance Mechanism." *Comparative Studies in Society and History* 24:264–273.

Kirshenblatt-Gimblett, B. 1974. "The Fable In Context—A Social Interactional Analysis Of Story-Telling Performance." In *Folklore: Performance and Communication,* ed. Dan Ben-Amos and Kenneth Goldstein, pp. 106–130. The Hague: Mouton.

Laserstein, H. 1926. *Der Griseldastoff in der Weltliteratur.* Weimar.

Laskier M. 1981. "Jewish Education in Morocco." *Pe'amim* 9:78–99.

Loomis, G. C. 1948. *White Magic: An Introduction to the Folklore of*

*Christian Legend.* Cambridge, Mass.: Medieval Academy of America.

Luethi, M. 1980. "Imitation and Anticipation in Folktales." In *Folklore on Two Continents: Essays in Honor of Linda Degh,* ed. N. Burlakof and C. Lindahl, pp. 3–12. Bloomington: Trickster Press.

Marcus, E. 1966. *From the Fountainhead.* Haifa: Israel Folktale Archives Publications Series.

Meir, O. 1977. "The Acting Characters in the Stories of the Talmud and the Midrash." Ph.D. diss., Hebrew University, Jerusalem.

Mills, M. A. 1982. "Cinderella Variant in The Context of Muslim Womens' Ritual." In *Cinderella Folklore Casebook,* ed. Alan Dundes, pp. 183–189. New York: Garland.

Mizrahi, H. 1967. *With Elders is Wisdom.* Haifa: Israel Folktale Archives Publications Series.

Nanah, R. 1958–1976. *A Treasure of Fairy-Tales.* Jerusalem: Privately published.

Nehmad, M. 1966. *The New Garment.* Haifa: Israel Folktale Archives Publications Series.

Noy, D. 1963a. *Folktales of Israel.* Chicago: University of Chicago Press.

———. 1963b. *Jefet Schwili Erzaehlt.* Berlin: Walter deGruyter.

———. 1964. *Seventy one Folktales from Moroccan Jews.* Jerusalem: Bi'tefutsot Ha'gola.

———. 1965. *The Beautiful Maiden and The Three Princes.* Tel-Aviv: Am-Oved.

———. 1966. *Seventy one Folktales from Tunisian Jews.* Jerusalem: Bi'tefutsot Ha'gola.

———. 1967. *Seventy one Folktales from Libyan Jews.* Jerusalem: Bi'tefutsot Ha'gola.

———. 1967. *A Tale for Each Month 1966.* Haifa: Israel Folktale Archives Publications Series.

———. 1967. "Folk Narratives About Blood Libel Among Jewish Ethnic Groups." *Mahanayim,* 110:32–51.

———. 1967. "Rabbi Shalom Shabazi in the folk legend of Yemenite Jews." In *Come Yemen,* ed. Y. Ratzhabi, pp. 106–133. Tel-Aviv.

———. 1971. *A Tale for Each Month 1970.* Haifa: Israel Folktale Archives Publications Series.

———. 1973. "Riddle in Wedding Ceremonies." *Mahanayim* 83: 64–71.

———. 1974. "Introduction." In *The Maiden Who Turned Into Flowers,* ed. Z. Qort, pp. 5–11. Tel-Aviv: Yehudith.

———. 1979. *A Tale for Each Month 1976–1977.* Jerusalem: Israel Folktale Archives Publications Series.

Patai, R. [1967] 1990. *The Hebrew Goddess.* Detroit: Wayne State University Press.

Propp, V. [1928] 1968, 1970. *Morphology of the Folktale.* Austin: University of Texas Press.

Raglan, L. 1936. *The Hero: A Study in Tradition, Myth and Drama.* London: Methuen.

# BIBLIOGRAPHY

Rank, O. 1959. *The Myth of the Birth of the Hero.* New York: Vintage.

Rooth, A. B. 1951. *The Cinderella Cycle.* Lund: C.W.K. Gleerup.

Schwarzbaum, H. 1968. *Studies in Jewish and World Folklore.* Berlin: Walter DeGruyter.

Seri, R. 1968. *The Holy Amulet.* Haifa: Israel Folktale Archives Publications Series.

Shenhar, A. and H. Bar-Itzhak. 1981. *Folktales From Beith-She'an.* Haifa: Haifa University Press. Pp. 160–164.

Shenhar, A. 1974. *A Tale For Each Month 1973.* Haifa: Israel Folktale Archives Publications Series.

Shenhar, A. 1982. *The Folk Narrative of Jewish Ethnic Groups.* Tel-Aviv: Cherikover. Pp. 134–145.

Siefkin, O. 1903. *Das geduldige Weib in der englischen Literatur bis auf Shakespeare.* Rathenow: M. Babenzien.

Stahl, A. 1976. *Stories of Faith and Morals.* Haifa: Israel Folktale Archives Publications Series.

Tarim, M. M. N.d. *Shevah Haim.* Casablanca: S.N.

*The Encyclopedia of Islam.* 1924. London: Leyden. 3:165–166.

Westermarck, E. 1968. *Ritual and Belief in Morocco.* New Hyde Park, N.Y.: University Books.

Widra, A. 1973. "Gawedy Gornicze." In *Literatura Ludowa,* 2:48–56.

Yeshiva, M. 1963. *Seven Folktales From Rumania.* Haifa: Israel Folktale Archives Publications Series.

# *Type Index*

The types refer to the Aarne-Thompson classification system, as expanded in the IFA Type Index. Most additions are Jewish oicotypes.

| AT | Page |
| --- | --- |
| 403 part IV | 145 |
| 405 | 145 |
| 506 | 69 |
| 506*C (IFA) | 68, 69 |
| 510 | 88 |
| 510 A | 143, 145 |
| 510*D (IFA) | 88 |
| 561 | 180 |
| *730 E (IFA) | 109 |
| *750 (IFA) | 106 |
| *776 (IFA) | 112 |
| 834 A | 166 |
| 837 | 154 |
| 874 | 53, 54 |
| 875 part IV | 131, 133, 148, 149 |
| 875 | 76, 131, 148 |
| 875 A | 148 |
| 875 E | 131, 132 |
| 887 | 35 |
| 922 | 76, 172 |
| 922*C (IFA) | 75, 173, 186 |
| 922*E | 154 |
| 922 I*b$_2$ (IFA) | 172 |
| 930 | 195 |
| 930*E (IFA) | 124 |
| 934 A | 124 |

# TYPE INDEX

# *Index*